GUIDE FOR CELEBRATING™
CONFIRMATION

PAUL TURNER

LTP

LITURGY
TRAINING
PUBLICATIONS

D1214448

Nihil Obstat
Very Reverend Daniel A. Smilanic, JCD
Vicar for Canonical Services
Archdiocese of Chicago
November 23, 2015

Imprimatur
Very Reverend Ronald Hicks
Vicar General
Archdiocese of Chicago
November 23, 2015

The Glossary definitions were written by Joseph DeGrocco and Dennis Smolarski.

This book was edited by Danielle A. Noe, MDIV. Victor R. Perez was the production editor, Anna Manhart was the designer, and Kari Nicholls was the production artist.

Interior images by Sandy Bertog 37; Karen Calloway 17, 31, 32, 38, 39, 40, 41, 42, 44, 49, 52, 55, 56, 58, 59, 67, 68, 69, 71; Martin Erspamer, OSB, vi, 6; Andrew Kennedy Lewis 15, 63, cover; Bishop Carl F. Mengeling 12; Danielle A. Noe 65; Jenny Reynish 2; I. Sanchez 50; John Zich 14, 16, 21, 22, 26, 46, 54, 60.

The photo on page 10 courtesy of the archives of Holy Comforter–St. Cyprian Parish, Washington, DC.

PREPARING PARISH WORSHIP™: GUIDE FOR CELEBRATING™ CONFIRMATION © 2016 Archdiocese of Chicago: Liturgy Training Publications, 3949 South Racine Avenue, Chicago, IL 60609, 1-800-933-1800; fax 1-800-933-7094; e-mail orders@ltp.org. All rights reserved. See our website at www.LTP.org.

Printed in the United States of America

20 19 18 17 16   1 2 3 4 5

Library of Congress Control Number: 2016932623

ISBN 978-1-61671-242-6

EGCC

CONTENTS

PREFACE

When the wind started blowing, Peter didn't think much of it. Caesarea was right on the coast. He only just arrived in town, but he had been staying in Joppa, a little further south, enjoying a breezy rooftop there. So he saw no reason to stop his lecture: "God anointed Jesus of Nazareth with the holy Spirit and power. He went about doing good and healing all those oppressed by the devil, for God was with him. We are witnesses of all that he did both in the country of the Jews and [in] Jerusalem. They put him to death by hanging him on a tree."[1]

Cornelius and his household fixed their eyes on Peter. Ears alert to his words, their mouths hung slack. Gentiles all, they were only somewhat familiar with Jewish traditions. But now they were hearing about a very special Jew, Jesus, who had gone about doing good.

Only four days ago Cornelius had seen a vision while praying. An angel said to him, "Send some men to Joppa and summon one Simon who is called Peter."[2] Cornelius dispatched Milites the soldier, and the servants Publius and Rectus. They went to Joppa. They located Peter's address. Standing outside the house, they shouted for him. Peter descended from the rooftop and spoke with them across the threshold of the front door. "I am the one you are looking for."[3] They explained themselves, and Peter invited them in. The next day Peter contacted the local Christian community in Joppa. Thomas, Simon, and Quintus traveled with him the next day to Caesarea—where he was now catechizing Cornelius, a centurion with the Italica Cohort, along with his relatives and close friends.

The wind grew stronger, but Cornelius concentrated on the words of Peter. "This man God raised [on] the third day and granted that he be visible."[4]

---

1 Acts of the Apostles 10:38–39.
2 Acts of the Apostles 10:5.
3 Acts of the Apostles 10:21.
4 Acts of the Apostles 10:40.

The window frames began to shake. The house creaked and yawned. The sound of the wind grew so furious that Cornelius' mother strained to hear what Peter had to say about Jesus: "He is the one appointed by God as judge of the living and the dead. To him all the prophets bear witness, that everyone who believes in him will receive forgiveness of sins through his name."[5]

With that, tongues as of fire appeared, parted, and came to rest on everyone in the room.[6] Peter had seen it all before. On Pentecost, Mary and the Apostles had had the same experience. Now it was happening again.

Peter understood it all, but the others did not. Cornelius remained calm, but Milites asked, "Are we under attack?" Publius said to Rectus, "I just repaired that window." Rectus said to Cornelius, "Shouldn't we get out of here?"

But then Cornelius started to praise God in a language no one knew. Other members of the household joined him. Publius, Rectus, and Cornelius fell to their knees.

Peter knew just what was happening. The Holy Spirit was back. Quintus said, "Peter, you haven't finished your speech yet. You worked hard on this." Simon said, "They haven't been baptized yet. They cannot receive the Holy Spirit." Thomas commanded Cornelius and his household, "You cannot speak in tongues until *after* you have been baptized." Milites thought this made sense. But along with everyone else in the house, he was swept up in the ecstasy of fresh belief.

Peter lowered his head and sighed. "Can anyone withhold the water for baptizing these people, who have received the holy Spirit even as we have?"[7] Then turning to his companions from Joppa, he gave the order: "Quintus, Simon and Thomas, baptize them in the name of Jesus Christ."

They stayed a few days. On the way home, the brothers who had come with Peter were still confounded. "How did this happen?" wondered Quintus. "They are Gentiles. They knew nothing about Christ before we got here. They

---

5 Acts of the Apostles 10:42–43.

6 See Acts of the Apostles 2:3.

7 Acts of the Apostles 10:47.

didn't even finish getting their instructions. No one tested their knowledge. They didn't spend hours helping their neighbor. They just showed up, prayed, and started speaking in tongues. I don't get it."

Peter thought back on his life with Jesus. He remembered the day Jesus had him haul ashore a miraculous catch of fish, the same day that Peter called himself a sinful man. He remembered the day he tried to correct Jesus, and Jesus called him Satan. He remembered the horrible day when he denied Jesus three times. He realized that if anyone did not deserve to experience the Holy Spirit, it was he. Yet Peter also remembered the sound of the wind on the Pentecost past.

"I don't get it either," Peter said. "Sometimes the Holy Spirit just comes to you. Like a gift."

WELCOME

Y ou are helping people prepare to celebrate the Sacrament of Confirmation. Perhaps you are doing this because you have experienced the Holy Spirit in your own life—in the quiet of your heart, in the power of your speech, or in the confidence of your faith. You believe that the Spirit dwells within you, and you are anxious to help others experience the same gifts. Thank you for offering your service to the Church.

> One of the highest responsibilities of the People of God is to prepare the baptized to receive the Sacrament of Confirmation.
>
> — *The Order of Confirmation*, 3

People present themselves for Confirmation because of various reasons. Some have received encouragement from their parents, who promised years ago at a Baptism to raise their child in the practice of the faith. Some thirst for the gifts of the Holy Spirit and want to experience a livelier faith. Some look forward to catechesis, in order to understand more about the Church that they love. Some want a reason to gather their family and rejoice in commonly shared values. Some have experienced a new love for the Church and are anxious to get more involved. Some are planning to make the event a highlight of the year for their parish community. Some anticipate meeting the bishop and receiving the inspiration that he can bring. Some have had an encounter with Jesus Christ in their prayer or in their communication with others. They seek a stronger friendship with him. There are many reasons why a celebration of Confirmation is being prepared, and they all show the action of the Holy Spirit in individuals, families, and parishes.

Those who receive this sacrament will immediately obtain certain priorities in the Church. Only those who have been confirmed are eligible to serve as a godparent for someone else's Baptism or Confirmation.[1] Only the

---

1 See *Code of Canon Law* (CCL), 874 §3.

confirmed can enter the novitiate of a religious order.[2] Only confirmed men can present themselves for Ordination to the diaconate or priesthood.[3] A Catholic is to be confirmed before getting married if Confirmation can be administered without grave inconvenience.[4] Clearly the Church regards the confirmed as precious members: role models and leaders.

All of this can happen because of the extraordinary gift that Confirmation bestows: the Holy Spirit. When the bishop confirms, he calls the name of the person in front of him and says these words: "Be sealed with the Gift of the Holy Spirit."[5] No other gift is greater. And it comes as a seal, a permanent embrace from God.

About This Book

This book will help you make preparations for the bestowal of this gift in your parish, whether you are a priest, a deacon, a catechist, a youth minister, a musician, a sponsor, a parent, a reader, a Communion minister, a server, an usher, a greeter, a sacristan—or a bishop. It will give you a background in the history and theology of Confirmation. It will walk you through the ceremony, so that you will know what to expect as you receive guidance for decisions you may need to make. It will also answer a number of questions that frequently arise concerning the age of Confirmation, appropriate catechesis, the ministers who play different roles, and the fruitful celebration of the liturgy.

Above all, this book hopes to reaffirm your own faith in Jesus Christ and in the Holy Spirit he promised to send. That Spirit came upon the Apostles at Pentecost, and upon Cornelius and his household even before they were baptized. The Holy Spirit is unpredictable, but the gifts of the Spirit always enable the faithful to proclaim the Gospel to all they meet—in deed and word, in service and prayer. As you prepare others for their encounter with the Holy Spirit, may you experience the same Sprit anew.

---

2 See CCL, 645 §1.
3 See CCL, 1033.
4 CCL, 1065.
5 *The Order of Confirmation,* 27.

About the Author

Paul Turner is pastor of St. Anthony Parish in Kansas City, Missouri. A priest of the Diocese of Kansas City–St. Joseph, he holds a doctorate in sacred theology from Sant'Anselmo in Rome.

His publications include *At the Supper of the Lamb* (Chicago: Liturgy Training Publications, 2011); *Glory in the Cross* (Collegeville: Liturgical Press, 2011); *ML Bulletin Inserts* (San Jose: Resource Publications, 2012); and *Celebrating Initiation: A Guide for Priests* (Chicago: World Library Publications, 2008). He is a regular contributor to *Worship* magazine's "The Amen Corner." He is a former President of the North American Academy of Liturgy, a member of Societas Liturgica and the Catholic Academy of Liturgy. He is a recipient of the Jubilate Deo Award (National Association of Pastoral Musicians) and the Frederick McManus Award (Federation of Diocesan Liturgical Commissions). He serves as a facilitator for the International Commission on English in the Liturgy.

The Theological and Historical Developments of Confirmation

"But you will receive power when the holy Spirit comes upon you,
and you will be my witnesses . . . to the ends of the earth."

—Acts of the Apostles 1:8

The New Testament

Each person's Confirmation is a sharing in the same gift of the Holy Spirit that the disciples received at Pentecost. The Apostles themselves shared the gift of the Spirit with others. Their successors, the bishops of the Church, continue this ministry today.

"Through the Sacrament of Confirmation the Apostles themselves and the Bishops, who are their successors, have handed on to the baptized the special gift of the Holy Spirit, promised by Christ the Lord and poured out upon the Apostles at Pentecost."[1]

Throughout his life, Jesus frequently promised his followers that he would send them the Holy Spirit.[2] He comforted his disciples with the word that the Holy Spirit would help them in time of persecution.[3] On the night before he died, Jesus made several promises at the Last Supper: He promised to send the Spirit of truth from the Father.[4] This Spirit would remain with them forever.[5] The Holy Spirit would help them be witnesses to Christ.[6] Then, after the Resurrection, mere moments before his Ascension, Jesus spoke his final words to his followers. He promised that they would receive power

---

1 Arturo Cardinal Tabera, Sacred Congregation for Divine Worship, "Decree," Prot. n. 800/71, August 22, 1971; as found in the newest publication of the OC.

2 For this collection of Gospel references, see the *Apostolic Constitution on the Sacrament of Confirmation* of Paul VI; OC, p. xvii.

3 See Luke 12:12.

4 See John 15:26.

5 See John 14:16.

6 See John 15:26.

1

through the coming of the Holy Spirit in order to bear witness.[7] These promises must have filled the disciples with anticipation.

Pentecost was one of several observances already on the Jewish liturgical calendar. Celebrated fifty days after Passover, it commemorated the gift of the commandments amid the fire and rumblings on Mount Sinai. In Jerusalem, on the occasion of the Jewish Pentecost following the final Passover of Jesus' life, the Holy Spirit descended in tongues as of fire upon the disciples gathered in an upper room. As their ancestors had received the Law from God on Mount Sinai, so these disciples received the Spirit of God in an upper room. They had suffered at the Crucifixion of Jesus and rejoiced at his Resurrection. They were surely nervous at his Ascension, so they had gathered in fear inside a room, uncertain of their mission and their future. The coming of the Holy Spirit changed all of that. Speaking clearly in languages unknown to them, the disciples boldly entered the streets of Jerusalem and brought the Gospel to the waiting world.

> "When the Advocate comes whom I will send you from the Father, . . . he will testify to me."
>
> —John 15:26

The Holy Spirit descended in tongues of fire upon the disciples.

Gifts of the Holy Spirit became manifest in other groups, including the household of Cornelius, whose story opens this book. Two other stories from Acts of the Apostles are especially significant. Before the conversion of Cornelius, Peter and John had traveled from Jerusalem to Samaria to lay hands on a group whose members had been baptized in the name of the Lord Jesus, and they received the Holy Spirit.[8] After the conversion of Cornelius, Paul discovered a group of twelve in Ephesus who had received only the baptism of John. Paul baptized them in the name of the Lord Jesus and laid hands on them. They

---

7 See Acts of the Apostles 1:8; Luke 24:49.

8 See Acts of the Apostles 8:14–17.

received the Holy Spirit— speaking in tongues and prophesying.[9] Traditionally the Catholic Church points to these two stories for the biblical origins of Confirmation: as in the past the Apostles imposed hands and imparted the Holy Spirit on those who had been previously baptized, so bishops today anoint with the Spirit those who were baptized at a younger age. The two biblical incidents in Samaria and Ephesus deal with Baptisms in special circumstances. It is reasonable to assume that hand laying and prayer for the Holy Spirit were acceptable features of normal Baptisms in the time of the Apostles.

Pentecost remains the foundational event for the Catholic Sacrament of Confirmation. On that day the followers of Jesus received the gift of the Holy Spirit. But this gift was not for their personal benefit. They were expected to use this gift—to preach the Gospel and tell all lands about Jesus Christ. The same applies to Confirmation today; the faithful receive the gift of the Holy Spirit with this purpose: to bear witness to Christ.

The Early Church

As Christianity spread, ministers began to include anointing among the initiation rites. The New Testament clearly shows that some Apostles laid hands on some of the newly baptized, but it never clearly tells about anyone anointing the baptized with oil. However, in speaking of Jesus' baptism, Peter told the household of Cornelius that God had anointed Jesus at that time with the Holy Spirit and with power.[10] In one of Paul's letters, he says that God anointed the followers of Christ and gave them the Spirit.[11] A letter of John says that his readers were anointed by the Holy One, and that this anointing has taught them.[12] In none of these instances is it clear that an actual physical anointing took place. Nonetheless, Scriptures such as these opened the door to the liturgical practice of anointing the baptized. This action put a special symbol into the initiation rites to express the Church's belief in the holiness of Christians.

The practice and interpretation of this anointing varied considerably in the early Church.[13] In Syria, for example, the anointing *preceded* Baptism.

---

9 See Acts of the Apostles 19:1–7.

10 See Acts of the Apostles 10:37–38.

11 See 2 Corinthians 1:21–22.

12 See 1 John 2:20, 27.

13 Background for this section can be found on the CD-ROM included with Paul Turner, *Ages of Initiation: The First Two Christian Millennia* (Collegeville: The Liturgical Press, 2000), chapter 2, section 3.

It carried meanings such as physical and spiritual healing, forgiveness, and power. In North Africa the anointing *followed* Baptism and carried priestly and messianic symbolism. In Rome there is evidence for two postbaptismal anointings with the same oil: a priest administered one to echo the metaphorical anointing of Christ, and a bishop administered the other in conjunction with hand laying. The bishop accompanied his anointing with a prayer for the coming of the Holy Spirit. Although the early Church witnessed a variable sequence of baptizing and anointing, both actions took place during the same extended ritual event.

> Since this anointing with Chrism aptly signifies the spiritual anointing of the Holy Spirit, who is given to the faithful, We wish to confirm its existence and importance.
>
> —Pope Paul VI, *Apostolic Constitution on the Sacrament of Confirmation*

In those days, the Church assigned no minimum age limit for people to receive this anointing. If people were eligible for Baptism, they could be anointed. Infants and adults alike experienced full initiation: Baptism, anointing, and even the receiving of Communion.

Throughout this period the anointing slowly became associated with the ministry of the bishop, but largely because he was also the ordinary minister of Baptism. Dioceses were much smaller in those days, so the bishop could preside over the complete initiation rites for most of his people. Also during this time he began to celebrate initiation on specific days, such as the annual observance of Easter.

Nonetheless, practical concerns intervened. A catechumen who lived some distance away from the cathedral may have been unable to travel for catechesis and worship. Another catechumen with a grave illness may have stirred concern that he or she would not live until the designated day for initiation. In some of those cases, a priest or a deacon conferred Baptism outside the usual time and place. They usually omitted the anointing because that action became increasingly associated with the ministry of the bishop. As early as the second or third century, the anointing that accompanied initiation was sometimes displaced from Baptism.

The anointing of the newly baptized carried various meanings in an effort to show forth the deep significance of Baptism.

The Term *Confirmation*

By the fourth and fifth centuries, the words *confirm* and *Confirmation* began to appear in Church correspondence and decrees.[14] By this time the regional variations in initiation rites were becoming more unified. The bishop's anointing became a feature of the postbaptismal ceremonies when he imposed hands on the newly baptized and prayed for the coming of the Holy Spirit. The ceremony was so impressive that people requested the bishop to perform it even in the instances when he was not present for the Baptism.

In those cases, when the bishop performed a ceremony for someone previously baptized by another minister, his action was called "Confirmation." Even though bishops anointed the newly baptized in centuries prior to this time, the action had not been called "Confirmation" until it separated from Baptism. The original sense of "Confirmation," therefore, seems to have been something authoritative: the bishop confirmed or affirmed the Baptism that someone else had performed. He did this through an anointing with chrism, an imposition of one or both hands, and an invocation of the Holy Spirit.

> The ordinary minister of Confirmation is the Bishop.
>
> —*The Order of Confirmation, 7*

In these early days of the new word's usage, it never described the anointing that the bishop gave immediately after a Baptism he had just performed. It applied only to a deferred anointing. In time that changed, but the reason why the word "Confirmation" is attached to this ceremony originally had to do with the bishop. The theology, therefore, had more to do with the responsibilities of a bishop and with the unity his role signified, rather than with baptismal initiation.

The Middle Ages

By the seventh century the liturgy of Confirmation had become more developed.[15] The word *Confirmation* was now used for the anointing performed by the bishop, even for candidates he had just baptized in the same initiation

---

14 Background for this section can be found on the CD-ROM included with *Ages of Initiation*, chapter 3.

15 Background for this section can be found on the CD-ROM included with *Ages of Initiation*, chapters 4–7.

rite. *The Gregorian Sacramentary* includes a prayer that the bishop offered on this occasion. He asked for those who were baptized to receive the spirit of wisdom and understanding, the spirit of counsel and fortitude, the spirit of knowledge and piety, and the spirit of fear of the Lord. This prayer was inspired by an Old Testament prophecy concerning a future descendant of Jesse, a king who would possess these traits in his spirit.[16] Christians believe that Jesus fulfilled this prophecy of Isaiah. By alluding to this passage in the Confirmation prayer, the bishop implied that all the baptized participate in the messianic mission of Jesus. He prayed for the coming of the Holy Spirit to help them fulfill their royal responsibilities in bringing about the Kingdom of God. The tradition of enumerating seven gifts of the Holy Spirit[17] can be traced to this prayer. They have a biblical foundation in Isaiah, but their sacramental meaning comes from a prayer first detected in the seventh-century Confirmation ceremony.

> The spirit of the LORD will rest upon him:
> a spirit of wisdom and of understanding.
> A spirit of counsel and of strength,
> a spirit of knowledge and of fear
> of the LORD,
> and his delight shall be the fear
> of the LORD.
>
> —Isaiah 11:2–3

By the eleventh century, entire orders of Confirmation were being compiled. Bishops confirmed in elaborate ceremonies prior to this time, and some early prayers are known, such as the one from the *Gelasian Sacramentary*. But there is no complete description of a Confirmation ceremony with prayers and rubrics until orders of Confirmation appeared. These probably fulfilled the practical needs for a bishop to remember how the ceremony should go, and for one diocese to share its procedures with another.

The Council of Lyons in 1215 included Confirmation among its list of seven sacraments, the first time the teaching office of the Church officially numbered seven sacraments. By this time the ceremony was almost always

The Seven Gifts of the Holy Spirit

• Wisdom
• Understanding
• Counsel
• Fortitude
• Knowledge
• Piety
• Fear of the Lord

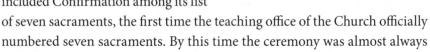

---

16 See Isaiah 11:2.

17 See *Catechism of the Catholic Church* (CCC), 1831.

administered apart from Baptism, so it was clearly a separate event. In the Eastern Rites, however, the priests who baptized also performed chrismation (Confirmation) in the same ceremony. They continued to celebrate the initiation rites in a single ceremony, judging that full initiation on one occasion was more important than reserving the anointing to the bishop later. Consequently, it was harder to see a distinction between the two sacraments in the East.

The Council of Florence established the matter and form of all the sacraments by legislating which substance and words were required for their valid administration. The Council certified that the matter for Confirmation was chrism made from oil and balsam, and the form was the words the bishop spoke to each candidate: "I sign you with the sign of the cross, and I confirm you with the chrism of salvation, in the name of the Father and of the Son and of the Holy Spirit."[18] Even though anointing developed after the biblical evidence of hand laying, anointing became the matter for confirmation.

The form for this sacrament reinforced the authoritative interpretation of Confirmation. The bishop simply declared what he was doing. His words of declaration formed a constitutive element of the sacrament. Its meaning was yoked to its minister. Confirmation was best understood as a ceremony that the bishop enacted.

Even when pontificals began to include the order of Confirmation, the ceremony was not grouped among the orders of other sacraments. Rather, it appeared as the first of the blessings offered by a bishop. Its liturgical connection to Baptism had long been lost, and the pontifical made scant effort to recover it.

Throughout this period infants were still permitted to receive Communion in the Roman Rite, and strong evidence shows that the practice was widespread. Infants received Communion at their Baptism; the priest offered both sacraments together. Infants would receive Confirmation in the same ceremony only if the bishop had just performed the Baptism. In those rare cases, infants received all three sacraments in the same liturgy.

More common, though, was the deferral of Confirmation to a later age. Consequently, these sacraments were administered over two separate events and in this sequence: Baptism with Communion for an infant, and then Confirmation when the bishop was available later. Throughout this time the

---

18 *Enchiridion Symbolorum Definitionum et Declarationum de rebus fidei et morum*, ed. Henricus Denzinger and Adolfus Schönmetzer (Barcelona: Herder, 1973), 1317.

word "initiation" only referred to the rituals performed at a *Baptism*. A Confirmation ceremony displaced some years from the baptismal rite was never called a sacrament of initiation—not until the twentieth century.

The age of candidates for Confirmation had everything to do with the availability of the bishop. Whenever he came to town, he confirmed those who had not yet received the sacrament—infants, children, and adults. However, in 1280 the Synod of Cologne set the minimum age at seven, and this eventually became canonical.

Slightly earlier, in 1215, the Fourth Lateran Council had required confession once a year after a person had reached the age of discretion. The Council did not require confession before Communion, nor did it defer Communion to the age of discretion, but it set up a rhythm that eventually led to those practices. Infants no longer received Communion, and the sequence of Confirmation and first Communion fluctuated considerably from the thirteenth century on.

Born anew by Baptism, the faithful are strengthened by the Sacrament of Confirmation and ultimately are sustained by the food of eternal life in the Eucharist.

—Paul VI, *Apostolic Constitution on the Sacrament of Confirmation*

With a higher age of Confirmation, the meaning of the word began to adopt a different nuance. The same word in Latin can also be translated as "strengthening." For those who had lived some years already as a baptized Christian, Confirmation strengthened them for service to the Gospel in the years ahead.

The theology of Confirmation at this time had a great deal to do with the ministry of the bishop. He was usually confirming those baptized by others, offering them the gifts of the Spirit while anointing them with chrism.

Post-Reformation

The Protestant Reformation uncovered and solidified divisions in Christian thought. Arguing from Biblical evidence, Martin Luther challenged the Catholic belief in seven sacraments, accepting only Baptism and the Lord's Supper in that sacred category of rituals. At the Council of Trent the bishops of the Catholic Church reasserted their belief in all seven, including Confirmation. Disputations arose between some of the most learned theologians of the day, and they inspired Christians on all sides to develop stronger catechesis for the faithful. Instructing children and adults required developing easily understandable arguments and dedicated classes. The invention of the printing press made catechesis of the faithful more possible than ever before.

One of the first fruits of the Council of Trent was its *Catechism of the Catholic Church* (1566). Work on this book was completed even before the liturgical reforms of the Council, which revealed how urgently the bishops wanted to educate the faithful. (Trent's *Order of Confirmation* would not be published until 1614, nearly fifty years later.) In the spirit of the times, catechetical preparation for Confirmation and first Communion expanded. Parishes started offering first Communion ceremonies by the end of the sixteenth century.[19] Although the age of children receiving first Communion fluctuated considerably, it gradually settled on youth who were about twelve years old.

The age of candidates for Confirmation continued to vary according to the availability of the bishop. However, the bishop no longer confirmed infants and young children. Once the children had received catechetical formation, and once the bishop had arrived for the ceremony, he confirmed the candidates whether or not they had celebrated their first Communion. The sequence of Confirmation and first Communion remained inconsistent.

> With regard to children, in the Latin Church the administration of Confirmation is generally delayed until about the seventh year. For pastoral reasons, however, especially to implant more deeply in the lives of the faithful complete obedience to Christ the Lord and a firm witnessing to him, the Conferences of Bishops may set an age that seems more suitable, so that this Sacrament is conferred at a more mature age, after appropriate formation.
>
> —*The Order of Confirmation*, 11

Although the theology of Confirmation remained strongly connected to the ministry of the bishop leading the flock of the baptized, the connections between confirmation and catechesis were growing for the first time.

Quam singulari

Pope Pius X encouraged the faithful to receive Communion frequently and favored sharing it with children at a younger age than was customary at the time. During his pontificate the Sacred Congregation on the Discipline of the

---

19 Background for this section can be found on the CD-ROM that is included with *Ages of Initiation*, chapters 9–10.

Sacraments released *Quam singulari* (1910), which effectively lowered the age of first Communion from twelve to seven years.[20] In reality, all the Congregation did was reaffirm the teaching of the Fourth Lateran Council, but its declaration changed the pastoral practice of first Communion ceremonies that a grassroots effort had been spearheading for centuries. *Quam singulari* said nothing about the age of candidates for Confirmation or its sequence with first Communion. It merely reopened the Communion table to young children. In practice, though, it established a sequence of sacraments in which Confirmation usually followed first Communion.

Patrick Cardinal O'Boyle presides over a Confirmation liturgy at St. Cyprian in Washington, DC, 1962.

Quam singulari also created a void for the sacramental preparation and celebration of preadolescents. Ever since the late sixteenth century, first Communion preparation and celebration at age twelve provided a conclusion to childhood religious formation and an impressive celebration to stress the importance of receiving Communion on Sundays. Now children were receiving Communion at a younger age, which weakened the incentive for them to remain in religious education.

Into that void stepped Confirmation. Throughout the twentieth century in many episcopal conferences around the world the age for the candidates of Confirmation began to rise. This adjustment fulfilled a catechetical desire to offer some ceremonial conclusion to religious education.

The actual requirements making a person eligible to receive Confirmation remained fairly minimal because the sacrament was still available to those who had reached the age of discretion. However, many

> Those who are to receive Confirmation must have already been baptized. Moreover, those faithful possessing the use of reason must be in the state of grace, be properly instructed, and be capable of renewing the baptismal promises.
>
> —*The Order of Confirmation*, 12

---

20 Background for this section can be found on the CD-ROM that is included with *Ages of Initiation*, chapter 12.

dioceses added considerably more expectations onto the preparation of candidates before bishops would confer the sacrament.

The theology of Confirmation began to change again. Instead of a celebration in which the bishop confirmed the Baptism of the faithful, it was popularly reinterpreted as a celebration in which the faithful confirmed their own faith. This was largely the interpretation accepted among Protestant Churches, and it gained wide acceptance among many Catholics.

The Second Vatican Council

Gathering in a more peaceful climate than the bishops experienced at the Council of Trent, the Catholic bishops of the world introduced a number of reforms at the Second Vatican Council (1962–1965). The *Constitution on the Sacred Liturgy*, the first document of the Council, set the stage for the Conciliar work that followed, while it launched the liturgical renewal of the Catholic Church. In treating the sacraments, the *Constitution* declared, "The rite of confirmation is also to be revised in order that the intimate connection of this sacrament with the whole of Christian initiation may stand out more clearly; for this reason it is fitting for candidates to renew their baptismal promises just before they

> The rite of confirmation is also to be revised in order that the intimate connection of this sacrament with the whole of Christian initiation may stand out more clearly; for this reason it is fitting for candidates to renew their baptismal promises just before they are confirmed.
>
> —*Constitution on the Sacred Liturgy*, 71

are confirmed."[21] The *Constitution* also favored celebrating Confirmation during Mass, which had not been the custom before. Confirmation had been celebrated during a kind of welcome ceremony for the bishop, but now it was recast as an action taking part within the celebration of the Eucharist. This introduced a Liturgy of the Word into the ceremony; participants would listen to Scripture readings at Confirmation for the very first time.

The first English translation of the ceremony became available in 1973. It was slightly amended shortly after the publication of the revised *Code of Canon Law* in 1983, and again after the revised translation of *The Roman Missal* in 2011. A completely revised English translation of the original 1971 *Ordo Confirmationis* became available in 2015. It completed another step in

---

21 *Constitution on the Sacred Liturgy* (CSL), 71.

the revision of the English translations of all liturgical books in accord with the principles articulated in *Liturgiam authenticam*.[22] The Vatican has never published a newer Latin edition of the order, but the translations include updating to match other liturgical books and canonical adjustments.

The Council aimed to change the theology of Confirmation once again, situating it more squarely among the initiation rites of the Church. This became clear in the ceremony not only with the renewal of baptismal promises, but also with the recommendation that the baptismal godparents serve again as Confirmation sponsors.[23] Furthermore, the rite makes no mention of a special Confirmation name, so it implies that the bishop administering the sacrament addresses each candidate using that person's baptismal name.[24]

One of the goals of the Second Vatican Council was to change the theology of Confirmation.

The post-Conciliar *Order of Confirmation* made a clarification regarding the matter of the sacrament and completely changed its form.[25] The traditional matter for Confirmation, chrism, remained the same. However, Pope Paul VI was aware of the arguments that the New Testament evidence for conferring the Holy Spirit involved hand laying, not anointing. He also knew that hand laying was greatly prized by the Eastern Rites. Consequently, he explicitly called for the one administering the sacrament to lay his hand on the head of the one being confirmed while anointing the forehead with his right thumb. This hand laying, and not the one that precedes it while reciting the Confirmation prayer over the group of candidates, includes the biblical imposition of hands, according to Paul VI. This effectively drew hand laying right into the administration of the sacrament, unifying the gesture with the anointing with chrism.

More significantly, the pope changed the words to be said in administering the sacrament. He found more expressive the formula used by the Byzantine Rite, so he adopted it for the Roman Rite. Formerly, the bishop made a declaration that he was confirming the person, but now he was to call the person's name and say, "Be sealed with the Gift of the Holy Spirit."[26]

---

22 See *Liturgiam authenticam*, 6.

23 See OC, 5.

24 See OC, 27.

25 See Pope Paul VI, *Apostolic Constitution of the Sacrament of Confirmation*.

26 OC, 9.

Other changes pertained to the authorized minister.[27] These brought several events to a climax. In 1929 Pope Pius XI gave bishops in Latin America authority to delegate priests to assist in the Confirmation of the vast numbers of newly baptized converts. This reestablished the practice of infant Confirmation in the Roman Rite. In 1946 the Sacred Congregation on the Discipline of the Sacraments gave priests authority to confirm any of the faithful in danger of death. The 1983 *Code of Canon Law* permitted priests to confirm any adult or child of catechetical age whom he baptized or received into the full communion of the Catholic Church.[28] The 1971 *Order of Confirmation* allowed a bishop to grant a priest the faculty to confirm when the bishop is unable to fulfill the responsibility. It also let the bishop associate priests with himself in administering the sacrament to large groups.[29]

All of this began to loosen the strict association between Confirmation and bishops in the Roman Rite. But nothing had a greater impact on the meaning and practice of Confirmation than the *Rite of Christian Initiation of Adults*, through which it became common for parishioners to see their priests administer the Sacrament of Confirmation at the Easter Vigil each year. That celebration has become the clearest example of how the Second Vatican Council recast the meaning of Confirmation to reaffirm its origins as a rite of initiation. It also explains why the Vatican has not yet encouraged raising the age of Confirmation, even though the practice has become widespread. The Confirmation of older children may cause people to interpret the sacrament as a graduation from religious education. Instead, the post-Conciliar *Order of Confirmation* assumes that children will be making their first Communion at the Confirmation Mass[30]—or that the children are *younger* than first Communion age.[31] The *Catechism of the Catholic*

> By this gift of the Holy Spirit the faithful are more fully conformed to Christ and are strengthened with the power to bear witness to Christ for the building up of his Body in faith and charity.
>
> — *The Order of Confirmation*, 2

---

27 Background for this section can be found on the CD-ROM included with *Ages of Initiation*, chapter 12.

28 See CCL, 883 §2 and 885 §2.

29 See OC, 8.

30 OC, 13: "The newly confirmed therefore participate in the Eucharist, which completes their Christian Initiation."

31 OC, 13: "If, however, the candidates for Confirmation are children who have not received the Most Holy Eucharist and are not being admitted to First Communion at this liturgical celebration or if other special circumstances so suggest, Confirmation should be conferred outside Mass."

The Order of Confirmation assumes that children will receive their first Communion at their Confirmation Mass.

Church states that "we must not confuse adult faith with the adult age of natural growth, nor forget that the baptismal grace is a grace of free, unmerited election and does not need 'ratification' to become effective."[32] Whenever facing the question of the best age for candidates of Confirmation, the Vatican has preferred a younger, not an older choice.

Still, because many dioceses in practice choose an age older than seven for Confirmation, the ceremony can resemble a graduation exercise. Apart from the renewal of baptismal promises, though, the words of the liturgical ceremony never endorse the idea that Confirmation is an achievement of Christian maturity, a personal acceptance of faith, or a permanent commitment to the Catholic Church. Instead, it reaffirms that Confirmation does what Pentecost did: it confers the gift of the Holy Spirit so that those who receive it may bear witness to the faith.[33]

---

32 CCC, 1308.

33 The newly revised ritual book for Confirmation was published in early 2016. The promulgation date for using the revised texts was Pentecost, 2016. The new ritual book is bilingual; English and Spanish found on facing pages. The rite includes "The Order for the Conferral of Confirmation within Mass" (chapter I), "The Order for the Conferral of Confirmation without Mass" (chapter II), "Those Things to Be Observed When Confirmation Is Conferred by an Extraordinary Minister" (chapter III), "Confirmation to Be Administered for a Sick Person in Danger of Death" (chapter IV), "Texts to Be Used in the Conferral of Confirmation" (chapter V), and "Text with Music for the Laying On of Hands" (appendix).

Preparing the Confirmation Liturgy

"Be sealed with the Gift of the Holy Spirit."

—*The Order of Confirmation*, 27

The Confirmation liturgy is going to leave a lasting impression on the minds of all who participate in it. Families will gather. Photos will be taken. Stories will be told. A careful preparation will bring rewards lasting far beyond Confirmation day.

In some dioceses the bishop celebrates all Confirmations at the cathedral church. This simplifies some of the preparation because the cathedral and diocesan personnel make most of the preparations, and they usually ensure that the ceremony flows slowly.

If the bishop is coming to your parish church, preparations become more complicated. He will probably have some preferences about how the ceremony should proceed. He may have one or more assistants who travel with him and know his customs. You may receive instructions weeks or months prior to his arrival to begin arranging the event. Often the anticipation of the bishop's arrival makes many people nervous, even the pastor. However, this tension may also draw out the very best that everyone has to offer.

The preparation team should involve key people from the parish and the diocese.

To prepare for the liturgy, you may need key people from the parish and the diocese: the pastor, the liturgist, the music director, the director of religious education, the youth minister, a representative from the bishop's office or from the diocesan office of divine worship. If the ceremony involves several parishes, all the pastors may wish to collaborate on the efforts. Your diocese probably has procedures in place for this event. If you can obtain the directives, you'll have a good idea of what is expected for you to do.

The liturgical ministers in your parish will probably do whatever they usually do for large celebrations such as Christmas and Easter. A choir may prepare special music. Extra greeters will be at the door. Sacristans will have sufficient vessels, bread, and wine for Communion. Decorations will be in place. Those who help maintain the building will see that it's clean, and that everything is in working order.

Sunday Mass is the paradigm for this celebration, but special arrangements will also be needed. Those to be confirmed, their sponsors, and families may need reserved seating. Some prefer to seat the candidates with their parents. It usually works best if they sit with their sponsors. But this also

Sunday Mass is the paradigm for the celebration of the Confirmation liturgy.

depends on the age of the candidates. Seats near the front make the best choice, and they can be reserved with signage or some decorative element. Someone may need to reserve a parking space for the bishop and let him know where to find it. Extra chairs may be set in the sanctuary for all the priests and deacons who will participate. The bishop may bring his own copy of *The Order of Confirmation*. If the presidential chair is not visible to the assembly, the bishop may bring or need you to provide a special chair for the occasion.[1] He may also bring his own chrism, but your sacristan should set out whatever the bishop needs to wash his hands after the anointing. Because this is a more thorough washing than the ceremonial one that takes place at every Mass, the bishop may need a large bowl and a pitcher with a good quantity of water. Some bishops use soap to wash up; others like a sliced lemon, which is more traditional but perhaps not as effective. A sufficiently large fresh hand towel should be placed nearby.

Even though the bishop will use *The Order of Confirmation* to confer the sacrament, he will still need a copy of *The Roman Missal* for the rest of the Mass. He may bring one, but he may use the one from your parish church. He, his master of ceremonies, or a sacristan may set the ribbons at the correct pages before the Mass begins.

---

1 See *Ceremonial of Bishops* (CB), 461. Traditionally, this is called a "faldstool," but the *Ceremonial* does not use the term.

The Roman Missal includes the collection of prayers for a Confirmation Mass. These are found about two-thirds of the way through the Missal in a section called "Ritual Masses." This section includes collections of prayers for many sacraments and other rituals. The first group is for the conferral of the sacraments of Christian initiation, and its fourth section includes the prayers for the conferral of Confirmation. These were composed for use at a Confirmation Mass, but they may also be used profitably in catechesis and meditation prior to the celebration.

The Missal has three sets of prayers for a Confirmation Mass. Set A includes an entrance antiphon; two options for the Collect; a Prayer over the Offerings; the

The Roman Missal includes the collection of prayers for the Confirmation Mass.

page number for the Prefaces of the Holy Spirit (from which one may be chosen, though neither is obligatory); special intercessions to be inserted into Eucharistic Prayers I, II, and III (whichever one is chosen); a Communion antiphon; a Prayer after Communion; and a Solemn Blessing for the end of Mass, as well as a Prayer over the People that may replace it. Set B offers another entrance antiphon, Collect, Prayer over the Offerings, Communion antiphon, and Prayer after Communion. Set C gives only one option for the three main presidential prayers (Collect, Prayer over the Offerings, and Prayer after Communion). Out of all these possibilities, the bishop may have a preference for which to use.

On some days the bishop may confirm during Mass, but he cannot use these prayers from the Mass of Confirmation. For example, any Holyday of Obligation; Sundays of Advent, Lent and Easter Time; Holy Thursday and the Sacred Paschal Triduum; any solemnity; All Souls' Day; Ash Wednesday; weekdays of Holy Week; and days in the Easter Octave. The most likely occurrence of a Confirmation liturgy on one of these days is a Sunday in Easter Time, a solemnity that falls on a weekday, or a day within the first week after Easter

> As a rule, Confirmation takes place within Mass so that the fundamental connection of this Sacrament with all of Christian Initiation, which reaches its culmination in the Communion of the Body and Blood of Christ, may stand out in a clearer light.
>
> —*The Order of Confirmation*, 13

Sunday.[2] In all those cases, the Mass of the day prevails with its Collect, Prayer over the Offerings, Preface, and Prayer after Communion. The bishop still confers the sacrament by using *The Order of Confirmation*, but throughout the rest of the Mass he offers the appropriate prayers from the Missal. As will be explained on subsequent pages, this may affect the readings as well.

The bishop may bring his own vestments, or he may wear vestments from your parish. Although most bishops offer this Mass wearing red vesture, they are permitted to wear white instead. If the Mass is one of the privileged Masses mentioned in the previous paragraph, a bishop wears the color associated with that day.

When all is prepared, you are ready to celebrate the Confirmation Mass.

The Introductory Rites

The entrance procession takes places as usual. *The Ceremonial of Bishops* lists the participating ministers in this order: the censer bearer, the cross bearer with seven or at least two other ministers carrying candles, the deacon with the *Book of the Gospels*, other deacons two by two, concelebrants two by two, the bishop, two deacons assisting him, and then other ministers who assist with the book, miter, and pastoral staff.[3] Concelebrants may need to be reminded that they precede the deacons who assist the bishop. (When a priest presides at a typical Mass, the deacon walks at his side or in front of him.)

Those to be confirmed may enter in the procession, or they may take their places in church informally before the Mass begins. There is no clear legislation on this. When the *General Instruction of the Roman Missal* discusses the entrance procession, it makes room for servers and "other ministers."[4] The *Directory for Masses with Children* permits children to join the entrance procession,[5] though it never explains when. Logically, if the candidates for Confirmation enter in procession, they would come between the servers and the person carrying the *Book of the Gospels*. Or, if no one is carrying that in procession, they would enter between the servers and the clergy. If there are ministers carrying incense, the cross, and candles, these always lead the procession. Others come after.

---

2 See CB, Appendix III.

3 See CB, 128.

4 *General Instruction of the Roman Missal* (GIRM), 120c.

5 See *Directory for Masses with Children* (DMC), 34.

Musicians may choose an entrance song from a wide variety of options, but it would be good for them to take note of the entrance antiphon from the Missal's ritual Mass of Confirmation. There are two options: Ezekiel 36:25–26 or Romans 5:5 with an allusion to Romans 8:11. The first is a prophecy that the Lord will pour clean water over the people and give them a new spirit. The second is Paul's affirmation that God's love has been poured into our hearts through the Spirit dwelling within us. The second antiphon fulfills the prophecy of the first.

The options for these antiphons are treated differently in the *Graduale Romanum*, which holds the primary collection of chant for the post-Conciliar liturgy. The Vatican approved the contents of this book primarily for communities that preserve the custom of singing Gregorian chant in Latin at a post-Vatican II Mass. It widens the sources of antiphons and psalms found in *The Roman Missal* and the *Lectionary for Mass*. Although others rarely consult the *Graduale*, it provides another view into the musical options for Mass.

Inside the *Graduale*, the first option for the entrance antiphon for Confirmation is a bit more expanded. It cites Ezekiel 36:23–26, and it offers a verse from the opening of Psalm 34 (33): "I will bless the LORD at all times; praise of him is always in my mouth." The gradual's second option is slightly different: Romans 5:5, 10, 11. It is paired with the opening verse from Psalm 103 (102): "Bless the LORD, O my soul, and all within me, his holy name." The gradual also says that the second option is to be used in Easter Time, whereas the first may be used throughout the rest of the liturgical year. The Missal does not make this distinction. Although the gradual is not well known among liturgical books, it provides useful information for psalm verses that can enhance the selections that the musicians make for congregational singing.

> When those to be confirmed are assembled with their sponsors and parents, and the whole gathering of the faithful, the Bishop approaches the sanctuary.
>
> —*The Order of Confirmation*, 34

Both of these antiphons were added to the ceremony after the Second Vatican Council because prior to that time there was no Mass at Confirmation. Some churches customarily opened the service with the antiphon "*Ecce sacerdos magnus*," or "Behold the great high priest." In this way the choir saluted the entrance of the bishop while all listened and watched attentively.

The first antiphon for the post-Conciliar Confirmation Mass also appears in the Missal for the Pentecost Vigil, where it was found in the pre-Conciliar Mass. The Missal's second entrance antiphon was added after the Council both to the Pentecost Vigil and to the Confirmation Masses as alternatives to the first.

If musicians have musical settings of the words of either of these antiphons, they may consider using them not only on Confirmation day but on Pentecost or other occasions throughout the year so that the community can include the songs in its repertoire.

After the Sign of the Cross, the bishop may greet the people with the words, "Peace be with you." The people's response is the same: "And with your spirit." His greeting wishes peace even as it alerts people about his special role for this unique occasion.

In place of the Penitential Act, the blessing and sprinkling of water may be used. The Missal permits this rite on Sundays because of the way it links Baptism with our regular observance of the Resurrection on the first day of the week. In practice, some have incorporated it on other occasions, such as a weekday Mass at a Catholic school. The baptismal connections make this act a tempting option for Confirmation liturgies. It would be most appropriate for those Confirmation Masses taking place on a Sunday.

The Gloria is sung at a Confirmation Mass. The Gloria could always be included on days of a special, solemn character,[6] but the third edition of the Missal now explicitly calls for it to be sung or recited at a Confirmation Mass. The revised English translation of *The Order of Confirmation* has added this information to that book for the first time.[7]

The Introductory Rites conclude with the appropriate Collect. When the bishop says, "Let us pray," each person in the community has a first opportunity in silence to formulate a prayer for the occasion. Each will probably pray for a specific candidate from the family or circle of friends. However, none of the Collects from the ritual Mass prays exclusively for the candidates. The bishop will be praying that the Holy Spirit will touch all gathered in assembly. No one should leave untouched.

---

6 See GIRM, 53.

7 See OC, 57.

The Liturgy of the Word

The proclamation of Scripture at a Confirmation ceremony was a welcome innovation from the Second Vatican Council. The Church's experience of this has been so positive that it is hard to believe that many sacraments were once administered without readings from the Bible, but Confirmation is a clear example. Now the community may hear from both the Old and New Testaments about the promise and fulfillment of the Holy Spirit's coming.

The Liturgy of the Word unfolds as it does at any Mass, although some elaborations can be made. For example, the Gospel procession may be accompanied by incense, candles, and "other symbols of reverence that may be customary."[8]

The Gospel procession may be more elaborate and take a longer route to highlight the significance of the movement.

These might include religious banners, bells, or additional candles. The procession may take a longer route to the ambo to highlight the significance of this movement. When a bishop presides, there may be one variation from the norm. After the deacon reads the Gospel and says, "The Gospel of the Lord," he may bring the book to the bishop, who kisses it. The bishop may then take the closed *Book of the Gospels* and use it to bless the people. Alternatively, the deacon may kiss the book himself as usual.[9] It would be courteous for the deacon to find out before the celebration if the bishop has a preference.

> [I]t is from the hearing of the word of God that the many-sided work of the Holy Spirit flows out upon the Church and upon each one of the baptized or confirmed and that the Lord's will is made known in the life of Christians.
>
> —*The Order of Confirmation*, 13

The readings are drawn from the Mass of the day or from the passages suggested among the ritual Masses for Confirmation in the Lectionary.[10] On days when the Confirmation Mass may not be used, the readings of the day

---

8 *Lectionary for Mass, Introduction*, 17.

9 See CB, 141.

10 These are found in the fourth volume of the Lectionary, # 763– 767. See also OC, 20 and 61–65.

prevail.[11] The number of readings is not specified, but customarily there are three, as on Sundays. If only two readings are desired, the Gospel is always one of them.

The First Reading

During Easter Time, it is customary to take the First Reading from the Acts of the Apostles. Otherwise, one of five Old Testament readings from the Lectionary may be chosen.

The readings are from the Confirmation liturgy or the Mass of the day.

- **Isaiah 11:1–4ab:** Christians believe that this messianic prophecy was fulfilled in the coming of Jesus Christ. The traditional seven gifts of the Holy Spirit mentioned in the Confirmation prayer find their origin here.

- **Isaiah 42:1–3:** The first of four servant songs from the last part of the Book of Isaiah opens with this prophecy. The servant will have the help of the Spirit to bring forth justice on the earth. Confirmation candidates will share in this call to the ministry of international justice.

- **Isaiah 61:1–3abcd, 6ab, 8c-9:** The Spirit of the Lord has anointed the servant to bring good news to the poor. Jesus quoted this passage in his inaugural appearance in Luke's account of the Gospel, and its appearance in the Confirmation liturgy lays expectations upon the candidates' future ministry with Christ.

- **Ezekiel 36:24–28:** To a people in exile, God promises to restore them to their own land and give them a new Spirit. Those to be confirmed can expect a new Spirit to revive their confidence in Christ. This passage may especially resonate with candidates who have struggled with their faith.

- **Joel 2:23a, 26—3:1–3a:** God promises to pour out the Spirit upon all people. Children shall prophesy. The elderly shall dream. Youth shall see visions. These promises are realized in the Sacrament of Confirmation, no matter the age of the candidate.

---

11 See CB, Appendix III.

The Second Reading

Among the New Testament readings, any of these could function as the Second Reading at the Confirmation Mass throughout the year. During Easter Time, though, one of the first five could be used as a First Reading in keeping with other liturgical books.

- **Acts of the Apostles 1:3–8:** In the days before his Ascension, Jesus makes one final promise to send the Holy Spirit to make the Apostles witnesses to the ends of the earth. Candidates for Confirmation will find this same message comforting and challenging, nerve-wracking and exciting.

- **Acts of the Apostles 2:1–6, 14, 22b–23, 32–33:** Here is the classic account of the first Christian Pentecost, the coming of the Holy Spirit upon the original followers of Christ. This passage is the source from which the Catholic Sacrament of Confirmation flows.

- **Acts of the Apostles 8:1bc, 4, 14–17:** Peter and John lay hands on a group baptized only in the name of the Lord Jesus, and these new believers receive the Holy Spirit. From about the fourth century, this was one of two biblical passages used to defend the ecclesial practice of bishops confirming as successors to the Apostles, who imposed hands on groups previously baptized.

- **Acts of the Apostles 10:1, 33–34a, 37–44:** The Holy Spirit falls upon Cornelius and his household while Peter catechizes them. The unpredictable arrival of the Holy Spirit shows how broadly the Apostles shared the gifts of the Spirit. The same Spirit comes in Confirmation today, even upon those who may feel unable to envision what the experience demands.

- **Acts of the Apostles 19:1b–6a:** Paul lays hands on members of a small group whom he has just baptized, and they receive the Holy Spirit. Together with the excerpt from Acts 8 cited above, this is the second of two Biblical passages that later commentators used to demonstrate the origins of the Confirmation ministry of bishops, successors to the Apostles. As the Apostles imposed hands on recently baptized Christians, so bishops anoint the baptized today in Confirmation.

- **Romans 5:1–2, 5–8:** The love of God has been poured into our hearts through the Holy Spirit whom we have received. The gift of the Holy Spirit received in Confirmation enables candidates to share the love of Christ with others. This sacrament should bear practical fruit in the lives of the candidates.

- **Romans 8:14–17:** Those led by the Spirit are children of God and joint heirs with Christ. As Jesus is the only begotten Son of God by his Incarnation, so Christians are adopted children of God through their Baptism. Confirmation bestows the gift of the Spirit through whom we all call God Father, together with—and at the command of—Jesus Christ.

- **Romans 8:26–27:** The Spirit intercedes for us with inexpressible groanings. At the first Christian Pentecost the Spirit allowed the Apostles to speak in unknown languages. Especially at Confirmation the Spirit comes to the aid of all those who do not know how to pray as they ought. The community may not experience the miracle of speaking in tongues, but candidates will receive the spiritual tools to profess their faith by word and deed to people of any culture.

- **1 Corinthians 12:4–13:** The one Spirit produces manifold gifts in the community. The fruits of Confirmation will differ from one candidate to the next, but all will share abundantly in the Holy Spirit. Candidates should prepare to share their unique gifts with the community, no matter how small they fear their contribution may be. It will surely build up the Body of Christ.

- **Galatians 5:16–17, 22–23a, 24–25:** The flesh and the Spirit are in contention, but those who forsake the flesh and live by the Spirit will enjoy more positive fruits such as love, joy, and peace. Candidates struggling to do God's will can find reassurance in the promise of the Holy Spirit who comes through this Confirmation. They can honestly acknowledge the temptations they face and draw confidence that the Spirit can help overcome them all.

- **Ephesians 1:3a, 4a, 13–19a:** Those who were chosen in Christ have been sealed with the promise of the Holy Spirit. All the baptized form a new chosen people, as is evident from the Rite of Election for those who have been catechumens. They are numbered among the elect, the people chosen for baptism. The words that the bishop speaks at Confirmation, "Be sealed with the gift of the Holy Spirit," are inspired by this passage.

- **Ephesians 4:1–6:** There is one body and one Spirit. One fruit of Confirmation is the unity it builds within the Body of Christ. Candidates can expect a greater participation in the family of the Church. The contributions that each one makes will strengthen the unity of the entire Body of Christ.

The Responsorial Psalm

The Lectionary lists psalms after the options for the Second Reading because in some celebrations only one reading is proclaimed before the Gospel. However, if two readings precede the Gospel, the psalm comes between the first two readings as it does at a typical Sunday Mass.

- **Psalm 22:23–24ab, 26–27, 28 and 31–32:** The singer proclaims God's name and also witnesses powerful results even to the ends of the earth. The psalm can be reinterpreted as a prophetic expression of the results of the first Christian Pentecost, and even the projected results of any particular Confirmation ceremony. The candidates will receive the Holy Spirit and bear witness that will draw attention not to themselves, but to God. When all the confirmed proclaim God's name, they proclaim the power of the Gospel to the ends of the earth.[12]

- **Psalm 23:1b-3a, 3bc-4, 5-6:** Easily recognized as the most popular of all 150 psalms, Psalm 23 proclaims the goodness of the Shepherd. At a Confirmation ceremony, the line that stands out most is, "My head you have anointed with oil." The anointing of the forehead is the primary action through which God imparts the gifts of the Spirit in this sacrament. When one's head is anointed with perfumed oil, one's heart swells to give thanks.

- **Psalm 96:1–2a, 2b–3, 9–10a, 11–12:** This psalm encourages the faithful to announce God's glory among all the nations. It serves as a prophecy for what happened at the first Christian Pentecost and challenges the candidates to accept their mission: Announce the Gospel to all the nations. Candidates living in a multicultural world will have this opportunity even at home. Others may sense more literally the summons to carry the Gospel to other lands.

---

12 Quotations in this section are taken from the Revised Grail Psalter, rather than the Lectionary. The United States Conference of Catholic Bishops has approved use of the Revised Grail in the liturgy and will include it in all future liturgical books in English.

- **Psalm 104:1ab and 24, 27–28, 30–31, 33–34:** This entire psalm praises God for the works of creation. The key verse is, "You send forth your spirit, and they are created, and you renew the face of the earth." This has been adapted into a petitionary refrain that worshippers sing at Mass on occasions such as Pentecost and Confirmation: "Lord, send out your Spirit, and renew the face of the earth." Whereas the psalm is grateful for the work of God's spirit in the creation of nature, the reworked refrain asks God to set the Spirit to recreate the spiritual lives of believers, who will join the task of developing the world according to the plan of God.

Our mission is to announce the Gospel to all nations.

- **Psalm 117:1bc, 2:** The shortest psalm in the Bible has the grandest theme. It summons all the nations to praise God. Either of two refrains may be paired with this psalm. One quotes Jesus' farewell address to the Apostles from Acts, calling them to be witnesses to the ends of the earth. The other refrain, "Alleluia," is offered because in the Bible this psalm is grouped with several others that include that word. The theme of universality again looks back to Pentecost and forward to the mission of the Confirmation candidates. On Pentecost the first Christians proclaimed the message to people from many nations gathered in Jerusalem, and at Confirmation the candidates are expected to continue that mission, bearing witness to the faith throughout all the world.

- **Psalm 145:2–3, 4–5, 8–9, 10–11, 15–16, 21:** In the original language, the first verse of this psalm begins with the first letter of the Hebrew alphabet, and each succeeding verse continues with the following letter. All these alphabetical verses form a theme and variation on the praise owed to God. The specific verses making this suitable for Confirmation come near the end: "[Your faithful ones] shall speak of the glory of your reign, and declare your mighty deeds." As the Apostles declared God's mighty deeds to their contemporaries, so shall the newly confirmed to all whom they meet.

To complete the official list of options, the *Graduale Romanum* offers a chant setting of Psalm 33:12 for the gradual of a Confirmation Mass: "Blessed the people whose God is the LORD, the people he has chosen as his heritage."

With this refrain it pairs verse 6 from the same psalm: "By the word of the Lord the heavens were made, by the breath of his mouth all host." The liturgy interprets that verse as a prophecy for the doctrine on the Holy Trinity because it mentions the Lord, the word and the breath of God all in one verse. If musicians wish, they could use a setting of this gradual in place a Responsorial Psalm after the First Reading.

Verse before the Gospel/Gospel Acclamation

For the verse before the Gospel, the Lectionary offers six options. Throughout most of the year, "Alleluia" serves as the Gospel Acclamation, but during Lent another acclamation praising Christ the Word of God replaces it. In either case, those preparing the music choose one verse from among the six options here.

- **John 14:16; John 15:26b, 27a; John 16:13a; 14:26b:** The first three options all come from Jesus' farewell discourse at the Last Supper in John's account of the Gospel. They include Jesus' repeated assurances to his disciples that he will send the Holy Spirit, first as an Advocate to be with them, second as a Spirit of truth to testify, and finally as a Spirit of truth who will guide and remind them of what Jesus told them. Each of these verses brings a note of assurance to those who may be fearful of the future demands that their life will place upon them.

- **Revelation 1:5a, 6a:** The verse from the Book of Revelation proclaims Jesus as a faithful witness and his followers as a kingdom of priests. Through Confirmation, those who were anointed into the common priesthood of the faithful at Baptism are anointed again to serve as witnesses with Christ. As a priestly people, those who are baptized and confirmed praise God's mighty deeds and offer sacrifice with Christ.

- The fifth option is the opening stanza of the sequence from Pentecost Sunday. It prays for the radiant light of the Holy Spirit. Its appearance here draws a natural connection between the events celebrated at Pentecost each liturgical year and the specific occasion of Confirmation. It also prays that any who experience darkness in the faith may find illumination by the gift of the Spirit.

- The final option is a traditional prayer for the coming of the Spirit to kindle the fire of love in the hearts of the faithful. This prayer deserves a place among those that Christians know by heart. The fire of the Spirit will be strongly kindled in the sacrament of Confirmation, but it can be set ablaze again and again through the spiritual discipline of prayer.

The *Graduale Romanum* offers options for the Gospel Acclamation as well. These could be sung as the verse to an acclamation that the people already know. The *Graduale* proposes Psalm 104:30, for which it offers two different musical settings, though any setting may be used. The verse comes from one of the options for the Responsorial Psalm: "You send forth your spirit, and they are created, and you renew the face of the earth." The gradual also suggests the opening stanza of the Pentecost sequence, which the Lectionary has proposed.

The Gospel

The proclamation of the Gospel is the highlight of the Liturgy of the Word. In this moment the words of the historical Jesus resonate afresh in the ears of the contemporary Church. These ancient words speak to human hearts of every age.

- **Matthew 5:1–12a:** The Beatitudes are the famous words that open the equally famous Sermon on the Mount. They formed a spiritual foundation upon which the first disciples could build their lives. One of the most frequent options in the Lectionary for rituals from Marriage to funerals, the Beatitudes are offered for consideration at Confirmation so that those who are renewing their discipleship in Christ can hear afresh the benefits of their faithful behavior. Jesus surely wished that his disciples of every generation would hear and heed these words.

- **Matthew 16:24–27:** Those who become disciples will accept a cross and follow Christ. The gifts of the Holy Spirit will renew the discipleship of the candidates, but they will face challenges on their way to glory. Those who accept the Cross of Christ embrace the responsibilities of life after Confirmation with a mature sense of mission.

- **Matthew 25:14–30:** Jesus' parable of the talents reminded his disciples that they should develop whatever gifts they have. In Confirmation, the candidates will be receiving a variety of gifts, and Christ will praise those who multiply them for the sake of the kingdom. Although many candidates have offered their gifts as evidence of their faith before Confirmation, this parable challenges them to share these gifts after receiving the sacrament.

- **Mark 1:9–11:** At Jesus' baptism, the Spirit descended upon him like a dove, and the Father's voice called him the beloved Son. In Acts, Peter refers to this event as the time when Jesus was anointed by the Spirit. Although there is no record of John the Baptist anointing Jesus with oil, the effect of the Spirit upon him anointed him metaphorically with a gleaming presence for mission. Candidates for Confirmation have been baptized in the name of the Trinity and have been numbered among the adopted children of God. Now they receive the anointing of the Spirit to begin their ministry anew in the church. The bishop will use oil in this anointing to drive the image home.

- **Luke 4:16–22a:** Appearing in the synagogue of his home town at the beginning of his ministry, Jesus reads passages from the prophecy of Isaiah and proclaims that he fulfills them. He is the anointed one of God, and his ministry to the poor, the captives and the blind is taken up by all those who are confirmed. The words of Isaiah were fulfilled in Jesus Christ, and they are fulfilled anew in all those who receive the anointing of the Spirit. At the Confirmation liturgy this passage is fulfilled in the hearing of all present.

- **Luke 8:4–10a, 11b–15:** Jesus' parable of the sower shows how some accepted his teaching, while others did not. Those who embrace his word will bear fruit through their perseverance. Confirmation is an important way that those who have listened to the Word of God receive the fruits of the Spirit due to their perseverance in faith and prayer. They are among the seeds cast upon good ground that will bear fruit for the benefit of the Church.

- **Luke 10:21–24:** Luke's account of the Gospel is sometimes called the Gospel of the Holy Spirit. Several times, as in this passage, Luke reports that Jesus was filled with the Holy Spirit as he set out to do something. Here Jesus, filled with the Spirit, praises God for revealing hidden things to the childlike. Those who celebrate Confirmation will be filled with the gifts and fruits of the Spirit, the wonders of God revealed to the childlike. They will perform great actions in the name of God.

- **John 7:37b–39:** Referring to the Spirit, Jesus promised that those who believe in him will have rivers of living water flow within them. Confirmation will bestow a full measure of the Spirit on the candidates, and the fruit of this sacrament will flow from them all the days of their lives. The results will be both internal and external. Those being confirmed will experience the power of the Spirit within them, and the Church will experience their sharing of the fruits of the Spirit.

- **John 14:15–17:** The remaining options for the Gospel all come from John's account of Jesus' farewell discourse at the Last Supper. Here, Jesus, who has acted as an Advocate for his followers, promises to ask the Father for another Advocate, the Spirit of truth who will remain with them. That Spirit came at Pentecost and comes again in the Sacrament of Confirmation. The very image of an "Advocate" should reassure the candidates that the sacrament is bestowed to bring them comfort, even as it challenges them to live the Gospel more faithfully and publicly.

- **John 14:23–26:** Jesus promises that after he is gone the Father will send the Advocate, the Holy Spirit, to teach the disciples and remind them of what Jesus said. That Holy Spirit came at Pentecost and comes again in Confirmation especially to those who yearn for the guidance that comes from God alone. Some candidates begin their preparation with questions about God and the Church. Even if they still harbor questions, the Advocate will help them face the mystery of God with resolve.

- **John 15:18–21, 26–27:** Jesus anticipates that his disciples will encounter opposition, but he promises that the Spirit, the Advocate, will help them testify to the truth. The newly confirmed cannot possibly realize all the difficult situations that they will face, especially the times when their faith will meet opposition. But they will have the assurance that on those days the Spirit, the Advocate, will stand at their side.

- **John 16:5–7, 12–13a:** Jesus seems aware that the disciples will feel lost after he dies, but he promises that the Spirit of truth, the Advocate, will guide them to all truth. That Spirit enlivened the testimony of the disciples at Pentecost and comes today to candidates who need the same Spirit of truth through the grace of Confirmation. Even those who ask penetrating questions about God, the Church, and the world will find guidance every step of the way as long as they seek the truth.

These last five choices are especially fitting if Confirmation is celebrated during Easter Time. The Lectionary does not explicitly set them aside for this purpose, but it reserves passages such as these for Sundays and weekdays during that period of the liturgical year. Choosing one of them for a Confirmation Mass during Easter Time will add uniformity to the Lectionary's seasonal voice. As will be seen below, even the communion antiphons suggest that these are especially fitting for celebrations when Lent is over.

The Order for the Conferral of Confirmation

The special feature of this liturgy is the conferral of the Sacrament of Confirmation. As with the celebration of many sacraments and rituals during Mass, the proceedings take place at the end of the Liturgy of the Word. The difference here (and in the Ordination rites) is that the candidates are named before the homily begins. In this way the conferral of Confirmation steps into the Liturgy of the Word, embracing the candidates and steering the homily toward the spiritual experience that they are about to share.

Calling the Names

Someone reads the names of the candidates.[13] This person may be the pastor, another priest, a deacon, or a catechist. The custom of each region may be honored. In some places, having the pastor read the names lends more dignity to the list. In other places, involving a catechist to do this verifies the credentials of the person who has assumed a leadership role in preparing the candidates for this day. Out of respect for the candidates, the person who reads this list should learn how to pronounce everyone's name correctly.

The tradition of having a special name for Confirmation is not part of the Church's current ritual.

The *Order of Confirmation* makes no mention about the custom of using a special name. Even if one will be used in conferring the sacrament, the person's baptismal name would more logically be used to introduce the ceremony. The name by which the family and friends know the candidate will inform everyone who is being called and summon the candidate to full attention.

If there are too many candidates to name them all without unduly prolonging the ceremony, their names may be omitted, and they may be identified as a group, such as "the candidates of this parish." This would be

---

[I]f possible, each of those to be confirmed is called by name and individually approaches the sanctuary; but if they are children, they are accompanied by one of their sponsors or parents and stand before the celebrant.

—*The Order of Confirmation*, 21

---

13 See OC, 21.

Preparing the Confirmation Liturgy 31

a sad loss. Most people do not mind waiting to hear their own name or the name of the one they love being read aloud. It personalizes the ceremony, and it prepares every single candidate for a personal encounter with the Holy Spirit.

As the name of each is read, the candidate approaches the sanctuary. If they are children, a sponsor or parent walks with them. If the group is large, and if the names are not being read, the bishop simply assigns them a suitable place. In practice, many parishes have the candidates remain at their places and stand there for the calling of their name. Then they sit down exactly where they were for the readings as the bishop delivers the homily.

One reason for having the candidates come forward is that the bishop will address them during the homily. Therefore, they may need special seating nearer the sanctuary for him to achieve eye contact. The rubrics imply that you are dealing with a fairly small number of candidates, but this is not always the case. However, if it is possible, having the candidates gathered in one place makes it easier for them to renew their baptismal promises as a group and to receive the upcoming Confirmation prayer offered by the bishop. It may make it easier for the bishop to make eye contact with them as he delivers his homily.

Wherever the candidates are at this moment, even though the bishop should ideally be able to see them, they should not block the view of all the others who participate in the ceremony. Other people will want to see the bishop too, and his words are going to have an impact not just on the candidates, but also on them. The rubrics never specify that the candidates sit for the homily, but it will be more comfortable for everyone if they do. If the group is small and the sanctuary sufficiently large, special seating could be arranged for them beforehand.

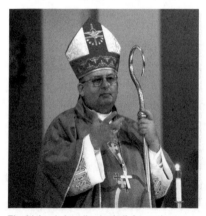
The bishop's homily sheds light on the readings and leads all present to a deeper understanding of Confirmation.

The Homily or Address

In his homily the bishop sheds light on the readings and leads all present to a deeper understanding of Confirmation. The rubrics say that he should be "brief."[14] A bishop's idea of brevity rarely matches that of the

---

14 OC, 22; see also CB, 462.

faithful. The point is that the length of his homily should not be disproportionate with the other liturgical elements of the celebration.

Some bishops have followed an old custom of turning the homily into a question and answer session—him asking the questions. The custom probably came from a time when people viewed Confirmation as a reward for religious education, and the questions the bishop asked served as the candidates' final exam. In place of any such an examination, the liturgy suggests that the bishop give an explanation of Confirmation in his homily, while exhorting the community to benefit from its celebration.

A sample homily appears in *The Order of Confirmation*. Some bishops use it; others adapt it; still others replace it entirely with one of their own. The sample homily gives the biblical background for the sacrament and its minister, affirms the coming gift of the Holy Spirit, makes the connection to life in Christ, and challenges the candidates to bear witness by the power of the Spirit. Normally any homily will explore most of these ideas, though sometimes the bishop has a specific message to deliver based on current events or on his contact with the candidates.

> The Bishop then gives a brief homily, by which, shedding light on the readings, he leads, as if by hand, those to be confirmed, their sponsors and parents, and the whole gathering of the faithful to a deeper understanding of the mystery of Confirmation.
>
> —*The Order of Confirmation*, 22

The Renewal of Baptismal Promises

The bishop leads the renewal of baptismal promises. These are the only questions the ritual has him ask the candidates. More important than quizzing them on their catechetical formation, he elicits from them a profession of faith. There is no recitation of the Creed at a Confirmation Mass. The renewal of baptismal promises replaces it, as it does in any Mass when Baptism is celebrated. Unlike the Easter Vigil, the faithful do not hold candles for the renewal of promises.

A similar renewal appears in *The Roman Missal* during the Easter Vigil. However, there are a few differences. For example, the Missal offers alternative sets of questions for the threefold renunciation. These are collapsed into one question at Confirmation. The candidates renounce Satan, his works, and "empty promises" all at once.

During the Easter Vigil the words for Satan's "empty promises" are his "empty show."[15] The traditional Latin word from the first set of these questions is sometimes translated "pomps." When the Rites of Baptism and Confirmation were being revised during the Second Vatican Council, the reformers made an effort to replace the Latin word *pompis* with *seductionibus*, a word taken from 2 Thessalonians 2:10.[16] Both in the *Rite of Baptism for Children* and in Easter Vigil text found in *The Roman Missal*, these two words remain in the alternative forms of the questions of renunciation. In the Confirmation ceremony, the word *seductionibus* was chosen as the only option. Therefore, you would expect the bishop to ask the Confirmation candidates to renounce "the lure of evil." However, the revised English translation has kept the words used in the first English translation at this point. It was thought by translators that children know all too well the meaning of "empty promises," which they may perhaps renounce even more readily than the "lure of evil."

The other significant difference in the renewal of promises comes in the questions pertaining to confessing faith. At Confirmation the final question from the Easter Vigil is expanded into two. This allows for the bishop to offer a fuller catechesis on the role of the Holy Spirit, and for the candidates to affirm more fully their belief. This question multiplies the titles of the Holy Spirit to include "Lord" and "giver of life," as in the Nicene Creed. The Spirit's role both at Pentecost and in this Confirmation ceremony is affirmed.

"Do you believe in the Holy Spirit,
the Lord, the giver of life,
who today through the Sacrament
   of Confirmation
is given to you in a special way
just as he was given to the Apostles on
   the day of Pentecost?"

— *The Order of Confirmation*, 23

The community longs to hear a confident response from the candidates throughout these questions. Naturally, many candidates will be nervous and inclined to speak timidly. Still, while preparing for this day, if they practice their response together and speak it loudly, their confidence will stir the hearts of the gathered faithful. The bishop gives his assent to this profession

---

15 *The Roman Missal*, the Easter Vigil, 55.

16 See *Consilium ad Exsequendam Constitutionem de Sacra Liturgia*, Schemata n. 210, De Rituali, 18, *Coetus a Studiis* XII: *De Rituali* I, 1 *martii* 1967.

of faith announcing how proud Christians are to profess it. His words will sound fitting if the candidates have sounded proud.

The assent of the bishop may be replaced with another formula or even a chant sung by the faithful. A refrain or acclamation about their belief in God makes the best choice. In this way, all may affirm their own faith. The *Ceremonial of Bishops* states this more strongly: it expects the community to respond to the bishop's statement with some acclamation or song.[17]

The Laying On of Hands

Before imposing hands on the candidates, the bishop invites all to a moment of silent prayer.[18] He stands, joins his hands, and faces the people. In some churches, when standing at his chair, the presider faces a side wall. He will be addressing the people, so he is to turn to look at them. This prayer demands the silent participation of the people he addresses. The silencing of instruments will help all the faithful, including the musicians, to concentrate. Other priests stand along with the bishop.

The bishop calls the candidates "adopted" sons and daughters, which is a reference to their Baptism. Jesus Christ is the only-begotten Son of God by his Incarnation, and his followers become adopted children of God by their Baptism.[19] The bishop prays that the Father will pour out the Holy Spirit to "confirm" the candidates—that is to strengthen them—with his gifts. The anointing will conform them more fully to Christ. This invitation contains quite a bit of catechesis on the meaning of Confirmation and explicitly helps the community to know what it is supposed to pray for in the ensuing silence.

The bishop "lays hands over" all the candidates, as do the priests.[20] In practice, they generally extend their arms forward, palms down, to "lay" hands over the entire group at once. In the rare ceremonies when only one individual is Confirmed, such as the case of an unconfirmed person in danger of death,[21] the bishop or priest places both his hands directly onto the head of the candidate. During this more ordinary ceremony under discussion, if the number of candidates is relatively small, the bishop could impose hands successively on the heads of each. This is what the *Ceremonial of Bishops*

---

17 See CB, 463.

18 See OC, 24.

19 See Galatians 3:26–4:7 and Ephesians 1:5, for example, as well as John 1:12 and 1 John 3:1.

20 OC, 25.

21 See *Pastoral Care of the Sick: Rites of Anointing and Viaticum* (PCS), 290; see also chapter IV in *The Order of Confirmation*.

implies when it says that the bishop "lays hands upon" the candidates.[22] The first English translation removed any ambiguity surrounding the gesture by adding an expression to the rubric, saying that the bishop and priests lay hands upon all the candidates "by extending their hands over them." This explanation does not exist in Latin and has been removed from the revised English translation. However, as Pope Paul VI indicated in his *Apostolic Constitution*, the real hand laying connecting with the Apostolic tradition comes not at this moment but during the anointing with chrism. This imposition of hands is similar to the gesture any priest uses when imparting a Solemn Blessing. For other liturgical prayers, he usually extends his arms wider, palms up, or facing each other. The very gesture indicates that this prayer is something out of the ordinary.

The bishop alone recites the prayer while his arms are extended. The words have existed in the Confirmation ceremony for over a thousand years. They incorporate the gifts of the Spirit first enumerated in Isaiah 11:2 as properties of the future Messiah. Christians have numbered them as the traditional seven gifts bestowed on all the faithful at their Confirmation.[23] The revised English translation of this prayer now matches the translation of the gifts in the *Catechism of the Catholic Church*. The words chosen to identify the final gift, "the fear of the Lord," have been controversial because they make it sound as though they promotes a terrified belief in a loveless, demanding God. However, the words "fear of the Lord" appear many times throughout the Bible in both Testaments, in books such as Proverbs and Psalms,[24] and Mary even alludes to them in

---

Almighty God, Father of our Lord Jesus Christ,
who brought these your servants to new birth by water and the Holy Spirit, freeing them from sin:
send upon them, O Lord, the Holy Spirit, the Paraclete;
give them the spirit of wisdom and understanding,
the spirit of counsel and fortitude,
the spirit of knowledge and piety;
fill them with the spirit of the fear of the Lord.
Through Christ our Lord.

—*The Order of Confirmation*, 25

---

22 See CB, 464.
23 See CCC, 1831.
24 For example, Proverbs 1:7 and Psalms 111:10.

her Magnificat.[25] They have more to do with a respect for the holiness of God, a sense for how different we humans are from the God who made us.

All answer "Amen" to the bishop's prayer. The congregation gives verbal assent to the silent prayer that they already made at his invitation.

The revised ritual book provides the text for the laying on of hands with chant notation in an appendix. It would be prudent for parish staffs to find out ahead of time if the bishop intends to chant this text.

The Anointing with Chrism

The actual administration of the sacrament follows in the anointing with chrism and its hand laying, along with the words of the bishop. This is the traditional moment during which Catholics understand that the Sacrament of Confirmation happens.

The bishop uses chrism. He has consecrated this oil at the annual Mass of Chrism in his diocese. Traditionally that event takes place on the morning of Holy Thursday, but many dioceses take advantage of the permission to host it on a day earlier in Holy Week or even the week before. During the same ceremony the bishop also blesses the oil of the sick and the oil of catechumens. He will share these oils with all the priests of the diocese, who will use them to administer the sacraments of the church in the upcoming year. (Deacons also may use the oil of catechumens

Clergy gather for the annual Chrism Mass at Holy Name Cathedral, Chicago, Illinois.

and the oil of chrism when they baptize.) If the local parish runs out of either of the oil of catechumens or the oil of the sick, or if a priest needs to anoint at a moment he does not have those oils at hand, he may bless any vegetable oil with the appropriate prayer to obtain a supply. However, a bishop and only a bishop consecrates chrism. If a parish runs out, it needs to get more from the original source.

At the Confirmation Mass, a deacon carries the vessel of chrism to the bishop.[26] Then the bishop approaches each candidate, or the candidates

---

25 See Luke 1:50.
26 See OC, 26.

approach him.[27] He needs one-to-one contact now with each of them. The logistics for this movement will be determined by the space available in the church and the number of candidates. Sometimes it is simpler for the bishop

to remain stationary while the candidates approach him one by one, as in a typical procession for receiving Communion. If the group is small enough and the space is wide enough, the candidates could stand still in a line, and the bishop could move from one to the next. Either way is acceptable.

The sponsor places his or her right hand on the shoulder of the candidate.

When the candidate and bishop face each other, the appropriate sponsor places his or her right hand on the shoulder of the candidate.[28] Although the right hand is specified, the particular shoulder is not. Again, logistics may determine if the sponsor places a hand on the right or left shoulder of the candidate. Standing in that position, the sponsor tells the bishop the candidate's name. Or the candidate tells the bishop his or her own name.

In practice, at many celebrations the candidates wear name tags. In this case, the bishop can read the name off the tag. This relieves him from straining to hear the name sometimes rendered by a soft-spoken voice. Names are quite varied, of course, and some bishops may prefer to see them rather than hear them. Candidates will help the bishop by positioning the name tag where he can see it, for example on front of a jacket, not on the shirt beneath it; not so high that long hair cascades over and obscures it; not so low that the bishop cannot locate it.

As indicated above, *The Order of Confirmation* makes no mention of a special Confirmation name. Neither does the *Code of Canon Law* nor the *Catechism of the Catholic Church*. The implication is that the candidates are confirmed with the same name by which they were baptized, uniting a primary symbol of the two sacraments. This is usually the name by which the candidate is known, and with which he or she answers calls and signs documents. That name has been sanctified in Baptism and is now consecrated in Confirmation.

---

27 See also CB, 466.

28 See also CB, 466.

Nonetheless, the tradition of having a Confirmation name persists. Some communities maintain it because it can connect the candidate with a role model saint, especially if the candidate's own baptismal name is not also that of a saint. However, Canon Law permits baptismal names that do not match those of saints. It only forbids a baptismal name "foreign to Christian sensibility."[29]

It is hard to defend an argument that a Confirmation candidate must be confirmed with the name of a saint. No universal legislation requires it. Candidates rarely use it ever again. There is great value to the practice of the bishop using the candidate's actual name, so that it may ever recall for that person the grace of Confirmation.

To perform the ceremony, the bishop dips the thumb of his right hand into the chrism, and with it he then traces the Sign of the Cross on the candidate's forehead while saying the sacramental formula: "**N.**, be sealed with the Gift of the Holy Spirit." The custom of the bishop using the thumb of his right hand is quite ancient, and the tradition endures.

While he does this, the bishop is to place the other fingers of his right hand on top of the candidate's head. This is the laying on of hands. Pope Paul VI says explicitly, "The Sacrament of Confirmation is conferred through the anointing with Chrism on the forehead, which is done by the laying on of the hand, and through the words, *Accipe signaculum Doni Spiritus Sancti*."[30] Paul used the singular of the word "hand" probably because there is significant evidence as far back as the second century that the bishop imposed only one hand in administering the rites of initiation.[31]

The bishop traces the Sign of the Cross with the sacred chrism on the candidate's forehead.

Some bishops may like to use more oil than what stays on their thumb, pouring some of it directly from a vessel onto the crown of the candidate's head so that it runs down a bit. Nothing forbids this, and it can be argued that this is a fuller sign of the importance of this sacrament. But the bishop must be

---

29 CCL, 855.

30 Pope Paul VI, *Apostolic Constitution on the Sacrament of Confirmation*.

31 For background see the CD-ROM included with *Ages of Initiation*, chapters 2–4, for example.

courteous not to get chrism in the candidate's eyes, and faithful to anoint the candidate's forehead using his thumb to trace the Sign of the Cross. The location on the head is important. During the Baptism of an infant, the priest or deacon anoints the crown of an infant's head with chrism while saying a different, nonsacramental formula: "[God] now anoints you with the chrism of salvation, / so that, united with his people, / you may remain for ever a member of Christ / who is Priest, Prophet, and King."[32] Although both sacraments call for the use of chrism, the minister, the words, and the location on the head are distinct. When a priest baptizes an adult or child of catechetical age, he also confirms that person, but the anointing with chrism on the crown of the head is omitted in order to avoid any potential confusion surrounding the two anointings.[33]

> Our Predecessor Innocent III wrote: "The anointing of the forehead with Chrism signifies the laying on of the hand, the other name for which is Confirmation, since through it the Holy Spirit is given for growth and strength."
>
> —Pope Paul VI, *Apostolic Constitution on the Sacrament of Confirmation*

The newly confirmed makes two responses in dialogue with the bishop. After the bishop administers chrism and says, "Be sealed with the Gift of the Holy Spirit," the newly confirmed answers, "Amen." The bishop then says, "Peace be with you," and the newly confirmed responds, "And with your spirit."[34] Young people are often nervous during a Confirmation ceremony at the moment they stand one on one in the presence of the bishop. Some of them may freeze. If they are carefully drilled before the ceremony, they can be kindly nudged during it. Preparation can happen during a catechetical session or in a special rehearsal inside the church. These two responses are important to the ritual, and bishops generally appreciate hearing the words confidently from every candidate.

After the anointing, a Sign of Peace is exchanged between the candidate and the bishop.

---

32 *Rite of Baptism for Children* (RBC), 125.
33 See *Rite of Christian Initiation of Adults* (RCIA), 228.
34 OC, 27.

If the number of candidates is large, or if for some other reason the bishop needs assistance in administering the sacrament, he may appoint priests to help. In this case, the deacon and servers bring the vessels of chrism to the bishop, and he personally presents them to the priests.[35] Sharing this ministry can promote the collegiality between the bishop and his priests, while showing courtesy to the members of the assembly who might otherwise endure an exceptionally lengthy ceremony. However, the bishop is the primary minister of the sacrament, and most people want him to perform the Confirmation. Some see this as a symptom of a culture

A "suitable chant" may be sung during the administration of the sacrament.

fixated on celebrities, but at its best it shows respect for the ministry of the bishop and the principle of unity that his office affords.

A "suitable chant"[36] may be sung during the administration of the sacrament. *The Order of Confirmation* makes no specific suggestions, and it is optional. Some people like singing here because it involves the entire assembly and helps engage them in the ceremony at a time when it can seem repetitive and distant, especially if the person whose Confirmation they came to witness was among the early recipients of the sacrament. However, others prefer having silence in the church while the bishop confirms. After all, each administration is personal and individual, and the words are important for each one of the candidates and for the people who have come to offer personal support. Another solution is for music to begin after the first few Confirmations are complete. Then, once everyone has heard the words, they can join in singing praise to God while the rest of the ceremony proceeds. Sometimes the bishop has a preference for silence; it would be prudent to secure his opinion in advance.

When the anointing is done, the bishop washes his hands. If any priests assisted, they wash their hands as well. Traditionally, water and sliced lemon is used because the lemon helps remove the oil from the hands. However, there is no legislation forbidding the use of soap and water if that works better. The

---

35 See OC, 28.
36 OC, 29.

bishop (and any priests) will also need a generous pitcher of water, a large bowl, and clean towels to dry their hands.

The administration of Confirmation is the solemn heart of this ceremony, and it concludes with a respectful washing. Throughout, people should have a sense of the awesome presence of the Holy Spirit, who graciously bestows gifts upon the members of the Body of Christ.

The administration of Confirmation is the solemn heart of the ceremony.

The Creed

There is no Creed at this Mass primarily because the renewal of baptismal promises takes its place. However, if the celebration of a sacrament such as Marriage takes place on a Saturday morning, for example, there is no Creed. The people usually recite the Creed at Mass on Sundays and solemnities, not at Masses including the administration of sacraments.

The Universal Prayer

Many people still refer to this part of the Mass as "the petitions" or the "Prayer of the Faithful," which is fine. The liturgical books are beginning to drop the designation "General Intercessions" because the petitions are not so much general in content as universal in scope.

As the celebrant, the bishop opens the Universal Prayer with a brief address to the people, and he concludes with a prayer to God. The petitions are then listed by a deacon or another minister. This minister addresses the people while announcing the needs, usually starting with a phrase such as "Let us pray for . . . " Then the people address God. The sample text provided in *The Order of Confirmation* is: "Lord, we ask you, hear our prayer." This is what makes this the prayer "of the faithful." They—and not the deacon or other minister—are the ones saying the prayers to God. The minister speaks to them; the faithful pray to God.

A set of sample petitions is included in *The Order of Confirmation*.[37] Other petitions may be used. The parish is still free to compose its own prayers, as at

---

37 See OC, 30.

any Mass. Reading the petitions from *The Order of Confirmation* is the simplest solution, but better is to prepare petitions that pertain more to the local community. Perhaps the candidates for Confirmation could suggest petitions they would like to include in the community's prayer this day. Part of their preparation for the celebration could be to think through the needs of the Church and the world. Petitions should cover four categories: the needs of the Church, public authorities and the salvation of the whole world, those burdened by any kind of difficulty, and the local community.[38] The Universal Prayer may be spoken or sung either in its entirety (verses and the response) or just the response. If the response is sung, instrumental music may be played softly under the petitions to segue into the response. A good cantor can lead this prayer.

> In Baptism, the newly baptized receive forgiveness of sins, adoption as children of God, and the character of Christ, by which they are made members of the Church and for the first time become sharers in the priesthood of their Savior (cf. 1 Peter 2:5, 9).
>
> —Paul VI, *Apostolic Constitution on the Sacrament of Confirmation*

The Liturgy of the Eucharist

Ushers usually do not take up a collection at a Confirmation Mass. However, in certain circumstances, they may. If, for example, the celebration is a regularly scheduled parish Mass, faithful members of the community will have come with envelopes ready to contribute to the support of the church. Outside a regular Sunday Mass, if the community wishes to lend financial support to a particular cause, a collection could take place. The funds could go to parish youth ministry, to a diocesan religious education office, or to a charity designated by those being confirmed, for example. A collection can expand the hearts of those who have come to worship, putting their desire for charity into action. If a collection is taken, the deacon, cantor, or commentator could announce its purpose for the benefit of those who may contribute.

The newly confirmed could also contribute to the collection. Young children may have their own kids' box of envelopes; older candidates may already be earning a salary at a part-time job. If they are contributing regularly on Sundays, they could do so at Confirmation as well.

---

38 See GIRM, 70.

For the procession of the gifts, some of those confirmed may join those who bring forward the offerings.[39] In many celebrations, only a group of the confirmed bring forward the offerings, but if others are designated for whatever reason, some of the newly confirmed may join them. The liturgy

The newly confirmed may bring up the gifts.

envisions that those carrying the gifts are among those who will be receiving Communion. As they carry forward the sacrifices of the people, they and the people will share in the fruits of their sacrifice at Communion.

The Prayer over the Offerings for the Confirmation Mass makes a petition for those who are newly confirmed. Thus, it prays more directly for this group than the Collect does. The first option prays that the newly confirmed may grow in bearing witness to Christ. The second option prays that they may constantly offer themselves to God and obtain an even greater outpouring of the Spirit. A third possibility prays that those who received the gift of the Holy Spirit may keep safe what they have received and come to eternal rewards. When Confirmation is celebrated on a day that requires a different set of Mass texts, this prayer gives way to the one for the appropriate day:

> Accept graciously these your servants, O Lord,
> together with your Only Begotten Son,
> so that, signed with his Cross and with a spiritual anointing,
> they may constantly offer themselves to you
> in union with him
> and merit each day a greater outpouring of your Spirit.[40]

Musicians may provide music for the Preparation of the Gifts. Instrumental, choir, or congregational music are all acceptable. The Missal does not include suggested texts for any antiphon at this time, but the Gradual does: Psalm 68:29–30. The revised Grail Psalms translates it this way: "Summon forth your might, O God; your might, O God, which you have

---

39 See OC, 31.
40 OC, 59.

shown for us. From your temple high in Jerusalem, kings will come to you bringing their tribute." In the pre-Conciliar liturgy, this antiphon was sung at the washing of the bishop's hands because in the Vulgate, the Latin translation of these verses begins with the same word that gives its name to this sacrament: *Confirma hoc Deus*. For a Confirmation during Lent, however, the Gradual recommends Psalm 119:47, 48. The revised Grail has this: "In your commands I have found my delight; these I have loved. I reach out to your commands, which I love, and ponder your statutes." It is unclear why this alternative passage is proposed, but perhaps the first was thought to be too glorious for Lent. In any event, musicians are not limited to these antiphons, but they may wish to consult them for ideas.

The Eucharistic Prayer

The Confirmation Mass usually includes a Preface of the Holy Spirit. The two options are found near the back of *The Roman Missal* in the ninth of the Votive Masses. The first recalls that Christ, after the Ascension, poured out the promised Holy Spirit upon God's adopted children. The second praises God for the manifold gifts of the Spirit that guide the governing of the Church. Through the Holy Spirit the Father aids the Church, whose members cry out in time of trouble and give thanks in time of joy.

On those occasions when Confirmation takes place while another Mass is being celebrated (for example, a Sunday in Easter Time), then the Preface of the season takes precedence.

The Preface opens the Eucharistic Prayer, and the bishop may choose either Prayer I, II, or III. He does not use Eucharistic Prayer IV because it has its own unchangeable Preface, and this Mass calls for a special one in every case.

Each of the possible Eucharistic Prayers includes a special intercession for the celebration of Confirmation. The wording is slightly different in each case, but each of them prays for the newly confirmed who have received the Holy Spirit, that God will keep this grace safely within them:[41]

> Remember also, Lord, your servants
> whom you have been pleased to confirm today
> by bestowing the Holy Spirit,
> and keep them in your grace.[42]

---

41 See OC, 58.

42 OC, 58; see the Mass for the Conferral of Confirmation A in *The Roman Missal*.

The Communion Rite

Communion may be administered under both kinds at this Mass.[43] In the United States, it is common to see Communion under both kinds at any Mass, so this will not be a surprise. In many churches globally, however, the cup is not offered to the faithful at Mass for a variety of reasons. For example, in some parts of the world wine is expensive and difficult to obtain. Especially in those churches, if possible, the cup may be shared with sponsors, parents, spouses, and catechists, as well as with any adults being confirmed. This permission for newly confirmed adults in no way excludes offering the Communion cup to newly confirmed children who have already received their first Communion, as is commonly practiced in many places. Even if they receive their first Communion at the Confirmation Mass, they may receive under both kinds.

Extraordinary ministers of Holy Communion may be needed for this occasion. The bishop, priests, and deacons who are present are all ordinary ministers of Communion, so they have the primary responsibility for offering Communion to the faithful. If having additional ministers would avoid a lengthy delay for those receiving Communion, they may be drawn from the parish's usual ministers, or from trained and commissioned catechists, family members, and sponsors of those being confirmed.

Music during the sharing of Communion should include congregational singing as usual. The Confirmation Mass suggests two antiphons based on biblical passages: Hebrews 6:4, which invites those who have shared in the Holy Spirit to rejoice; and Psalm 34:6, 9, which invites the faithful to look toward

Music during the sharing of Communion should include congregational singing.

God and be radiant, and to taste and see that the Lord is good.[44] The first of these especially fits this celebration in which some of the faithful share in the Holy Spirit at Confirmation; and the second seems to correspond with the

---

43 See OC, 32; see also the CB, 470.
44 See OC, 58 and 59.

opening of the Pentecost Sequence, which may also serve as the verse for the Gospel Acclamation. As the sequence prays for the radiant light of the Holy Spirit, so the psalm sees radiance on the faces of the faithful.

The *Graduale Romanum* offers a completely different set of antiphons for Communion, along with verses. The first is a collection of verses from the Beatitudes (Matthew 5:8, 9, 10), one of the recommended Gospel accounts for the Confirmation Mass. It suggests coupling with this refrain verses from Psalm 34, which supplies one of the Communion antiphons in the Missal.

The second option is Matthew 25:20–21, from the parable of the talents, another of suggestions for the Gospel at a Confirmation Mass. With this the *Gradual* pairs Psalm 119, which supplies some other texts for the Confirmation Mass.

The *Gradual's* third suggestion for the Communion antiphon is Matthew 16:24, where Jesus invites those who wish to follow him to take up a cross. Once again, it comes from a suggested Gospel for the occasion. With this antiphon the *Gradual* suggests very specific verses from Psalm 34; namely, 2, 3, 4, 6, 9, 12, 13, 14, and 15.

The *Gradual* does not restrict most of these antiphons to any part of the liturgical year, but the last two are for use outside of Lent. They come from the farewell discourse of John's account of the Gospel, which is proclaimed during Sundays and weekdays of Easter Time. In John 14:18, Jesus promises that he will not leave the disciples orphans. This is paired with Psalm 122, a processional psalm into the Temple of Jerusalem. The *Gradual's* last Communion antiphon collates John 15:26 with 16:14, 17:1 and 17:5, in which Jesus promises the Spirit and affirms that the Father will glorify him. Psalm 78 is recommended for the verses, a lengthy historical psalm telling of God's mighty deeds. It includes a verse about humans eating the bread of angels,[45] which has made it a favorite for Communion and for Eucharistic adoration.

All the *Gradual's* Communion antiphons come from Gospel accounts that may be proclaimed at a Confirmation Mass, and they give additional evidence to a practice that even the Missal occasionally observes: the Communion song is a good time to sing a verse from the Gospel of the day. If any of these Gospel accounts are chosen for the Confirmation Mass, then the appropriate Communion antiphon makes a fine choice. However, musicians are free to choose other songs if they wish. Often they resort to words

---

45 See Psalm 78:25.

about the Eucharist, but songs about the Holy Spirit or service to the Church also make good choices.

The bishop has three options for the Prayer after Communion. Like the Prayers over the Offerings, the first two are especially directed toward the newly confirmed. The first asks God to accompany them with his blessing, to gladden the Church by their holiness, and to evangelize through their works and charity. The second asks God to instruct them in the fullness of the divine law that they may show the world the freedom of the children of God and exercise their prophetic mission by the holiness of their lives. The third choice asks God to pour out the Spirit of love upon the entire assembly that they may experience unity. When Confirmation is celebrated on a day that requires its own Mass formula, this prayer is replaced by the appropriate one.

> Accompany with your blessing
> from this day forward, O Lord,
> those who have been anointed with the
> Holy Spirit.
>
> —Prayer after Communion,
> *The Order of Confirmation*, 58

Concluding Rites

A Solemn Blessing closes the Confirmation Mass. A threefold blessing of this kind connects historically to the ministry of the bishop. This category of blessing originated in the Middle Ages as a unique aspect of the Masses for which a bishop presided.

The bishop greets the people as usual ("The Lord be with you"). After everyone responds, the deacon or the bishop himself says, "Bow down for the blessing." The congregation is supposed to bow from the waist at this point. The newly confirmed could be instructed beforehand to bow and look down, not up, and to listen carefully to the words of the bishop, answering "Amen" to the three parts of the blessing. It's harder than it seems because the three parts do not conclude with a formula such as "for ever and ever" that more naturally cues an "Amen," and while bowing, no one is making eye contact with the bishop. But a rehearsal of the candidates sometime before the Mass can lead to a fulsome response.

The newly confirmed are dismissed into the world to share the gifts of the Holy Spirit that they have received, to proclaim Christ, and to spread charity to all they meet.

This Solemn Blessing refers to one member of the Holy Trinity in each of its three parts, and the bishop directs his words explicitly to the newly confirmed.[46] He asks that God the Father will bless them and keep them worthy of his love. He hopes that the Son will confirm (strengthen) them in the confession of the true faith. He prays that the Spirit will bless them and lead them blameless and united into the joy of the kingdom.

The bishop then blesses everyone with the usual formula. In doing so, however, he makes three Signs of the Cross, one for each member of the Trinity. This distinguishes his blessing from the single Sign of the Cross that the faithful more commonly witness their priest give.

As an alternative to the Solemn Blessing, the bishop may offer a Prayer over the People. The structure is different. Instead of three statements addressed to the newly confirmed, the bishop offers one prayer addressed to God.[47] He asks God to confirm

He later promised his disciples that the Holy Spirit would help them also to bear fearless witness to their faith.

—Paul VI, *Apostolic Constitution on the Sacrament of Confirmation*

46 See OC, 33.
47 See OC, 33.

(strengthen) the action of this ceremony, and preserve the gifts of the Holy Spirit in the hearts of the faithful. He also prays that all will profess to the world their belief in Christ and fulfill his commands.

Confirmation prepares us to go into the world to share the gifts of the Holy Spirit, to proclaim Christ, and to spread charity to all we meet.

With that, the deacon or in his absence the bishop dismisses the people with one of the usual formulas, and all answer "Thanks be to God." The dismissal at Mass always is more of a sending than a dismissing. That is, it does not simply end the ceremony inside the building; it sends people out into the world. At a Confirmation Mass, this is particularly important because the newly confirmed have just been endowed with gifts of the Holy Spirit for this purpose. They may think that the ceremony is a kind of graduation, an endpoint of their religious education. But it is a beginning. With this dismissal they go into the world to share the gifts of the Holy Spirit that they have received, to proclaim Christ and to spread charity to all they meet.

Frequently Asked Questions

Age and Sequence

1. Why does the age of candidates for Confirmation differ across the country and around the world?

The Vatican authorizes conferences of bishops around the world to establish their own age for Confirmation within certain guidelines and with the approval of the Apostolic See. Some conferences prefer a younger age, which helps ensure that more children actually receive the sacrament. A younger age also strengthens Confirmation's relationship with the Baptism of children. Other conferences prefer a later age to allow greater formation in faith.

A conference may choose a single age or a range of ages. The United States has one of the largest ranges in the world—from the age of discretion to about age sixteen. The country is too diverse to settle on a single age or even a smaller range. American bishops may choose an age for their diocese within that range—or they may adopt the entire range for the greatest flexibility. Neighboring dioceses are supposed to work together so that the age does not much vary in the region, but often the discrepancy in the age of candidates across diocesan boundaries is noticeable and confusing.

> With regard to children, in the Latin Church the administration of Confirmation is generally delayed until about the seventh year. For pastoral reasons, however, especially to implant more deeply in the lives of the faithful complete obedience to Christ the Lord and a firm witnessing to him, the Conferences of Bishops may set an age that seems more suitable, so that this Sacrament is conferred at a more mature age, after appropriate formation.
>
> —*The Order of Confirmation*, 11

2. What does "restored order" mean?

The term "restored order" refers to the celebration of Confirmation prior to the candidate's first Communion. In the early Church it was common for people of any age to be baptized, confirmed, and welcomed to the Communion table all in the same initiation ceremony. Some dioceses promote that infants and young children receive the sacraments in that same order, even when they are not celebrated on a single occasion: Baptism, then Confirmation, and then first Communion. Some dioceses even offer children their First Communion at the Confirmation Mass. This practice "restores" a more original "order" of the three sacraments of initiation.

3. Why do some children receive all three initiation sacraments at once?

Unbaptized children of catechetical age whose parents wish them to prepare for Baptism are to be enrolled in the catechumenate.[1] When their preparation is complete, they celebrate all three sacraments of initiation in the same ceremony, usually at the Easter Vigil. "Catechetical age" is about the same as the age of preparing for first Reconciliation and first Communion. If an

Unbaptized children of catechetical age are enrolled in the catechumenate and receive all three sacraments at once.

unbaptized child has reached the age when baptized children are preparing for first Communion, that child will celebrate Baptism, Confirmation, and first Communion all in the same ceremony, even if the child is below the diocesan age for the Confirmation of those baptized as infants. This practice is observed for the benefit of the child. The priest who baptizes the child has the faculty to confirm from the law itself; he does not obtain it from the bishop. Those who have the faculty must use it for the sake of the child's spiritual well-being.[2]

Not all young children have this privilege of receiving the three sacraments together because the bishop is still the ordinary minister of Confirmation for those baptized Catholic at a younger age. This preserves part of his ministry.

In the Eastern Rites, every priest who baptizes an infant gives Confirmation (chrismation) as well. He also offers the infant first Communion

1 See RCIA, 252.
2 See CCL, 883 §2 and 885 §2.

in the same ceremony. In the early history of Confirmation, the Latin Rite assigned the sacrament to the responsibility of the bishop, while the Eastern Rites assigned it to priests. The different practices still endure today.

4.　Is a child ever confirmed right after Baptism?

In the Roman Rite any priest may confirm any child who is in danger of death, even an infant.[3] If a priest needs to perform an emergency Baptism for anyone whose life is in danger, he may bring chrism and confirm at the same time. He does not need the bishop's permission. A deacon or layperson who conducts an emergency Baptism cannot confirm.

As indicated above, priests of the Eastern Rites commonly confirm the infants they baptize. In the Roman Rite, an unbaptized child of catechetical age enters the catechumenate and receives Confirmation right after Baptism. The priest who baptizes must confirm the child in the same ceremony. Normally he performs these ceremonies at the Easter Vigil, but for a good reason he may baptize and confirm an adult or child of catechetical age on a different occasion.[4]

5.　Can a person be confirmed more than once?

No Catholic can receive the Sacrament of Confirmation more than once. The sacrament carries a "character" or indelible spiritual mark because its gift of the Holy Spirit is unique and permanent.[5] Other sacraments imparting a character are Baptism and Holy Orders.

Some validly baptized Christians being received into the full communion of the Catholic Church were confirmed in another Christian community, such as the Episcopalians, Lutherans, or Methodists. Even though Christian communities may share the name of a ceremony called "Confirmation," the meanings are different. The Catholic Church regards Confirmation as a sacrament, and requires that it be administered by a validly ordained bishop or priest. Hence, someone who experienced Confirmation in a different Christian community still receives the Sacrament of Confirmation when becoming a Catholic. Every baptized person may receive the Catholic Sacrament of Confirmation only once.

3　See CCC, 1307; CCL, 891, 883 §3.
4　See RCIA, 26-30.
5　See CCC, 1304.

Ministers and Roles

1. Why is the minister of Confirmation usually a bishop?

In the Roman Rite, the bishop is the ordinary minister of Confirmation. This has long been the tradition, even though there are exceptions. Bishops are successors to the Apostles. As the Apostles imposed hands and imparted the Holy Spirit in the early days of the Church, so bishops do today. When a bishop administers Confirmation, he joins a continuum from the earliest days of the Church's ministry. He also exercises his role as a source of unity for the diocese. He entrusts the ministry of Baptism to priests and deacons to meet these

Under certain circumstances, a priest may confirm.

sacramental needs of the faithful more easily. But he serves as shepherd of the entire flock when they approach him for the Sacrament of Confirmation.

Under certain circumstances, a priest may confirm. He confirms an adult or child of catechetical age whom he baptizes or receives into the full communion of the Catholic Church. In other circumstances when one or more people baptized as infants need to be confirmed, a bishop is the normal minister, but he may delegate a priest to confirm in his stead. Or he may delegate a priest to assist him when the number of candidates at one ceremony is large. A priest may always confirm in danger of a candidate's death. In all these cases the priest serves as an extraordinary minister of Confirmation because the bishop is the ordinary minister. Only bishops and priests may confirm.

2. Who may be a Confirmation sponsor?

The ideal Confirmation sponsor is the baptismal godparent. The person who accepted responsibility for assisting parents in raising the child in the practice of the faith should step forward again at Confirmation. Both *The Order of Confirmation* and the *Catechism of the Catholic Church* make this recommendation.[6]

The sponsor may be chosen by the candidate or the candidate's family, but the pastor should ensure that the proper qualifications are met. The godparent should be sufficiently mature, be a member of the Catholic Church who has received the three sacraments of initiation, and not be impeded by law to fulfill a sponsor's responsibilities.[7] Canon Law establishes certain requirements for baptismal godparents that also apply to Confirmation sponsors: they must be at least sixteen years of age, though there are exceptions; and they must not be the parent of the one being confirmed. The first version of the *Rite of Confirmation* published after the Second Vatican Council permitted parents to present their own children for Confirmation in place of having a sponsor, but this no longer appears in *The Order of Confirmation* because of the more recent legislation in the *Code of Canon Law* that forbids parents to serve as sponsors.[8]

Sponsors must be at least sixteen, be mature in the faith, and may not be a parent of the child being confirmed.

3. What roles are essential in the Confirmation liturgy?

The bishop usually presides for the Confirmation Mass and serves as the minister of the sacrament. He preaches the homily and leads the community in prayer.

Priests may assist the bishop. Commonly the pastor and other priests working in the parishes of those being confirmed will concelebrate. During the conferral of the sacrament, they extend their hands over the candidates together with the bishop, while the bishop alone recites the Confirmation prayer.[9] The bishop may ask one or more priests to assist him in administering

---

6 See OC, 5; CCC, 1311.
7 See OC, 5.
8 See CCL, 874 §1.
9 See OC, 25.

the sacrament, especially if the group is large.[10] Normally, though, the bishop desires to confirm all the candidates, and the candidates and their families want the bishop to administer the sacrament for them.

Deacons may assist the bishop as they may do at any of his Masses; for example, a deacon proclaims the Gospel and a deacon may invite the community to exchange a Sign of Peace. At the start of the conferral of Confirmation, a deacon may present the candidates by name.[11] He carries the chrism to the bishop.[12] He may read the petitions of the Universal Prayer.[13] At the end of the Mass he may command the community to bow down for the blessing.[14]

Sponsors may accompany young candidates when they first stand before the bishop.[15] As the bishop prepares to anoint each candidate, the sponsor places his or her right hand on the shoulder of the candidate, and tells the bishop the candidate's name.[16] Sponsors may participate in Communion under both kinds.[17]

Catechists may also serve in the ceremony. One of them may read the names of the candidates at the beginning of the ceremony in place of the deacon.[18] Catechists may receive Communion under both kinds.[19]

Catehcists may read the names of the candidates in place of the deacon.

Parents may stand with young children as their names are called.[20] They would appropriately receive Communion under both kinds.[21]

The candidates themselves probably best focus on just being candidates. Sometimes their catechists may ask one or more of them to perform some other role in the liturgy—reader, cantor, or even

10 See OC, 28.
11 See OC, 21.
12 See OC, 26.
13 See OC, 30.
14 See OC, 33.
15 See OC, 21.
16 See OC, 26.
17 See OC, 32.
18 See OC, 21.
19 See OC, 32.
20 See OC, 21.
21 See OC, 32.

extraordinary minister of Holy Communion. However, the only liturgical role that *The Order of Confirmation* invites the newly confirmed to share is assisting with the procession of the gifts.[22] The other roles would more appropriately be carried out by other members of the community.

4. How is the whole parish involved in Confirmation?

Anyone in the parish can become involved in preparing candidates and celebrating the sacrament with them. It's a good idea for interested parties to visit with someone on the pastoral staff, watch for announcements in the bulletin or on the website, and listen to invitations at church.

Everyone can help spread the word about the opportunity to be confirmed. As members become aware of other members who have not yet celebrated the sacrament, they can encourage them to register for sacramental preparation. The sacrament will foster their own spiritual benefit, and it will prosper the good of the entire community, which will profit from an outflowing of gifts of the Holy Spirit.

Catechists often need assistance for the preparation sessions they offer. Whatever time volunteers can give may help lighten a catechist's load. If the parish is short on catechists, interested members may inquire what they should do to become qualified to serve.

Sometimes the candidates need help finding someone to serve as a sponsor. Their baptismal godparents may be unable to continue, or sadly may have died. The family may not know many other people in the community. Those who walk as a sponsor provide a great benefit for the candidates and their families.

> To a large extent it is the responsibility of Christian parents to show concern for the initiation of their children to the sacramental life both by forming and gradually increasing a spirit of faith in the children and, sometimes with the help of their instructors who are responsible for catechetical formation, by preparing them for the fruitful reception of the Sacraments of Confirmation and the Eucharist. The duty of the parents is also expressed by their active participation in the celebration of the Sacraments.
>
> —*The Order of Confirmation*, 3

As members of the parish become aware of the names of the candidates undergoing formation, they may include them in their prayers and come to know their families. Parents usually need support in the sometimes difficult

---

22 See OC, 31.

task of encouraging young people to participate in Confirmation preparation. The support they receive from their brothers and sisters in the community will give fuel to parents' faith and strengthen the guidance they give.

During the Confirmation liturgy, members of the parish may be able to participate in the celebration, especially trained ministers among the members of the candidates' families or friends confirmed the previous year. They may take on specific liturgical roles or offer prayerful support from the pew. Full, conscious, and active participation is the right and duty of all the faithful. Especially at a time like this, the faithful can give life to the liturgy through participating in the songs and responses, by praying with sincerity of heart, and by rejoicing in the sharing of the gifts of the Spirit. Nevertheless, parishioners should ask about attending the Confirmation liturgy. If the number of candidates is large, the parish church may not be able to accommodate many more people beyond the families, close friends, and sponsors of the candidates.

Family members who are trained and properly commissioned liturgical ministers may serve during the Confirmation liturgy.

The parish may appreciate having extra ushers and greeters on hand, or people to plan, set up, and clean up a reception after the liturgy.

Afterward, members of the parish can stay in touch with those who were confirmed. They can encourage continued participation in parish life and help find ways to put the new gifts of the Spirit at work in the community.

5. How is Confirmation an opportunity for evangelization?

The very nature of this sacrament is to endow candidates with the gifts of the Holy Spirit needed to bear witness to Jesus Christ. It is all about evangelization. The celebration should result in a recommitment to faith and purpose. Often the prerequisites for Confirmation include a number of service hours to the community. But the real service should come *after* Confirmation. Filled with the gifts of the Spirit as the first disciples at Pentecost, the newly confirmed go into the world to speak the language of faith in words and deeds that others will understand.

Confirmation preparation can promote service opportunities that will last beyond the date of confirmation. When candidates start making a personal connection with others, when they learn the joy of sharing their faith, they will become natural evangelizers. They can invite others to join them in prayer and in service, and to participate in future preparation for this sacrament.

The Confirmation liturgy will speak to the hearts of some participants who have not made a commitment to Christ or whose faith has lapsed. If the parish has good greeters at the door, they can be sure everyone feels at home.

The songleader's introductory comments can extend a welcome to all visitors and give an invitation for them to return. If your parish is printing a worship aid with the music and responses of the people, be sure to include the contact information about the parish: name, address, website, e-mail, and the names of current staff.

Good greeters can ensure that everyone feels welcomed.

Catechesis

1.   How is the RCIA a model for youth initiation?

The Catholic Church has two different liturgical orders for Baptism: one for infants and one for adults. The one for adults also pertains to children who have reached catechetical age, or first Communion age. The Baptism of infants is far more common than the Baptism of adults in the Catholic Church. Those baptized as infants approach the other initiation sacraments (Confirmation and First Communion) according to the guidelines of their Catholic diocese. Those baptized according to the adult formula receive all three sacraments in the same ceremony, usually at the Easter Vigil. The description of the pertinent liturgies and the broad expectations for catechesis are found in the *Rite of Christian Initiation of Adults* (RCIA).

The RCIA has inspired a number of imitative approaches that provide both catechesis and liturgical celebration to candidates for other sacraments. The RCIA's blend of liturgy and catechesis is emulated by those who assist in the preparation for other sacraments.

Some Confirmation preparation materials reflect this influence. For example, as candidates for Baptism are presented to the community in the RCIA's Rite of Acceptance into the Order of Catechumens, so candidates for

Confirmation are sometimes presented to the Sunday assembly to receive its prayer. *The Order of Confirmation* does not imagine preliminary rites such as this, but many parishes have informally created a ceremony to alert the community about its members in preparation and to solicit their prayerful support.

Although the imitation of some of the RCIA's processes is admirable, there is a great difference between catechumens who have never been baptized and baptized candidates preparing for Confirmation. The first are anticipating membership in the Body of Christ; the second are already adopted children of God through Baptism, now awaiting the special outpouring of the Holy Spirit.

The Catholic Church has two different liturgical orders for Baptism: one for infants and one for adults.

Catechesis for adult Baptism usually takes four different forms.[23] First, it includes "a suitable catechesis"[24] that is gradual and complete in presenting what the Church teaches. This catechesis invites the catechumens into a sense of wonder before the mystery of God. Second, it promotes familiarity with the Christian way of life. In this life, new members to the Christian community will adopt the customs and values demonstrated and expected by other Christians. Third, preparation is marked by suitable liturgical rites that help the catechumens become more at home with Christian worship patterns. Fourth, they learn how to work actively with

---

23 See RCIA, 75.
24 RCIA, 75.1.

others to spread the Gospel. The combination of these four forms builds a well-rounded Christian.

These same four catechetical methods can profitably help shape formation for other sacraments, including Confirmation. Candidates should (1) learn about their faith, (2) live it in concert with other Christians, (3) develop their abilities at Christian prayer, and (4) put their faith into actions of service and evangelization. Blending catechesis and liturgy will help candidates prepare for a worthy celebration of Confirmation. These methods can be helpful even though confirmation candidates presumably are not being introduced to Christianity, but have lived it thus far.

2.   How can we best stress that Confirmation is more initiation than graduation?

It is hard, especially if the age of the candidates approaches the age when many parents no longer encourage the formal religious education of their children. Confirmation does not mark the end of religious formation, but a new beginning of evangelization. It has less to do with the past, more to do with the future. Besides, all of us need continued religious formation throughout our lives. The celebration of Confirmation focuses in a different direction. It will equip the candidates with the gifts of the Spirit necessary for spreading the Gospel.

> It will be appropriate to adapt the plan for the catechumenate for those who were baptized in infancy and only in adulthood approach Confirmation.
>
> —*The Order of Confirmation*, 3

Part of Confirmation preparation can stress the purpose of these gifts. They are given to help the candidates witness to Christ, not for their personal enjoyment. If Confirmation preparation has been long and stressful, candidates will have a hard time grasping that what they are about to receive is a "gift." It will feel like a reward for much hard work. But the reward is not just for them. The gift is for the community.

Candidates can spend some time preparing for the sacrament by reflecting on how the Holy Spirit has been working in their lives so far, and how they might use those gifts for others. They may be able to compare their personal development of other gifts—in sports, the arts, relationships, or education. If they are using their gifts in new ways that make a difference in the lives of others, they will more easily envision how the gifts of the Spirit will awaken in them new abilities to serve the Church.

The goal of preparation is not merely receiving the Sacrament of Confirmation, but using it. The end point is not the Confirmation ceremony, but the daily life that extends beyond.

3.   Where does chrism come from?

The bishop consecrates chrism at the annual Chrism Mass at the cathedral during or shortly before Holy Week. Traditionally chrism is made from a blend of olive oil and balsam, a sweet-smelling liquid fragrance. Today, because these elements may be difficult to obtain in some parts of the world, any vegetable oil and any perfume may be used. But many dioceses prefer to mix the traditional ingredients.

During the Chrism Mass the bishop also blesses the oil of the sick and the oil of catechumens. Priests anoint the sick who have some serious illness or are in some perilous condition of ill health. Priests and deacons may use the oil of catechumens to anoint infants just before their Baptism and catechumens at any time during their formation. If he runs out, a priest may bless his own new supply of either of these oils.

However, only a bishop may consecrate chrism. Whenever a priest or deacon uses chrism in the Rite of Baptism, he uses an oil that comes from the hand of the bishop. It is one way that the bishop's ministry unifies the diocese. Chrism is also used to anoint the hands of priests at their Ordination and to anoint a new altar and the walls of a new church. It is used in each of the sacraments that can be received only once: Baptism, Confirmation, and Ordination. Once a person has been anointed with chrism, the results are permanent.

Usually the diocesan Chrism Mass is open to the public. Candidates for Confirmation may attend. In this way they may witness the consecration of the chrism that the bishop will use to anoint them. The ceremony is usually impressive, highlighted by the mixing of perfume and oil and the solemn prayer of consecration over the chrism.

4.   Does each candidate choose a Confirmation name?

Some dioceses and parishes maintain the custom of having candidates choose a Confirmation name, but there is no universal or national legislation requiring it. The rite seems to presume that the bishop will use the candidate's baptismal name in order to draw a closer connection between these two sacraments of initiation. Still, many candidates select the name of a saint who becomes a model of holiness and virtue for them. There is no universal requirement that a *baptismal* name be that of a saint, so the Church makes no such universal requirement for Confirmation. Still, diocesan guidelines may vary, and those preparing the candidates should learn what they are.

5. How can we best prepare candidates for the ceremony?

The best preparation is the understanding the candidates receive about the meaning of Confirmation. Some catechists try to stress that those being confirmed personally affirms the faith that others professed on their behalf when they were baptized as infants. Other catechists tell candidates that their Confirmation constitutes a permanent commitment to the Catholic Church. But *The Order of Confirmation* does not stress these ideas. It does include a renewal of baptismal promises, but candidates have already professed their faith every Sunday that they have come to Mass. Those who have already received Communion answer "Amen" in faith whenever the minister has said to them, "The Body of Christ" and "The Blood of Christ." These candidates have been making professions of faith on their own throughout their conscious lives.

Now they are receiving gifts of the Spirit to empower their witness to the world. When they focus on this meaning, the readings and prayers of the Confirmation ceremony will make more sense.

To prepare for the celebration, catechists can rehearse the candidates to make them comfortable. Some logistics need to be addressed. Where and when

The prayers of the Confirmation liturgy will make more sense if preparation is focused upon receiving the gifts of the Holy Spirit to empower their witness to the world.

will they walk? Where do they sit? Where do they stand? Where will the bishop be for the conferral of the sacrament? The design of the church, the number of candidates, and other local factors will help answer these questions.

Candidates will also benefit from learning about other aspects of the ceremony. At the beginning they will hear the bishop give an unfamiliar greeting after the Sign of the Cross—not "The Lord be with you," but "Peace be with you." Their response remains the same: "And with your spirit." Rehearsing this dialogue will help them feel more at home as the ceremony begins.

In place of professing the Creed, candidates renew their baptismal promises at this Mass. Part of the preparation for Confirmation can include a meditation on these promises, so that the candidates know what they mean. From time to time a catechist could lead them in a renewal of these statements during a preparation session. In this way, the candidates come to know the content of the promises, deepen their faith, and proclaim it with confidence.

The bishop will need to know each candidate's name. The sponsor is expected to give the bishop this information, but in some ceremonies the candidates wear a name tag. If this is the case, they should place the name tag where the bishop can easily read it, and help him see it when they step into his presence.

Candidates will also be asked to make two statements during the conferral of the sacrament. When the bishop calls each by name, he will say, "Be sealed with the gift of the Holy Spirit." Each candidate needs to answer, "Amen." Then the bishop will say, "Peace be with you." The candidate responds, "And with your spirit." It will help the bishop and the entire flow of the ceremony if the candidates are schooled in this, ready to respond in confidence and gratitude.

Near the end of the Mass the bishop may use a longer form of the blessing. If so, the deacon or the bishop himself will command, "Bow down for the blessing." All present should bow from the waist. Candidates could practice this posture for prayer at some catechetical sessions. Practice will help them feel at home and attentive as they listen to the bishop's words.

If the bishop is using the threefold solemn blessing, the candidates and all present should answer "Amen" to each petition. A rehearsal may help them feel comfortable with this prayer and to make a robust response. The whole ceremony is about gaining confidence to bear witness to Christ. If the candidates gain confidence in making the responses during the ceremony, they will start out on solid ground.

Candidates are encouraged to celebrate the Sacrament of Reconciliation just prior to their Confirmation.[25] In this way they enter the ceremony cleansed of sin and open to the gifts of the Spirit.

Preparing the Liturgy

1. When is it appropriate to celebrate Confirmation outside of Mass?

It is recommended that Confirmation take place during Mass so that the newly confirmed complete their Christian initiation with the Eucharist.[26] However, circumstances may arise in which the ceremony takes place during a Liturgy of the Word. At times the bishop's schedule or his health may interfere with his ability to preside for a lengthy service. Or the candidates may not yet have received their First Communion, and it would be less meaningful to continue with a Liturgy of the Eucharist.

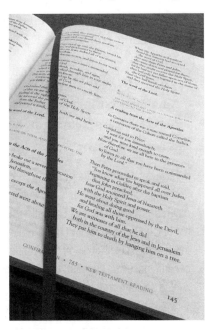

If Confirmation is celebrated outside of Mass, at least one reading should come from the ritual Mass.

The ceremony without Mass is fairly simple. All gather, and as the bishop and the ministers approach the sanctuary, all sing an appropriate song.[27] The bishop greets the people and says the Collect. He may use any prayer from the Mass of Confirmation in *The Roman Missal*, but another one is proposed for this celebration that concludes with a shorter formula than usual: "Through Christ our Lord." It subtly indicates that the opening of this ceremony differs from the opening of the Eucharist.

For the Liturgy of the Word, at least one reading is proclaimed from the section of the Lectionary devoted to the Confirmation Mass.[28] Two or three readings may be proclaimed in imitation of a typical Liturgy of the

---

25 See CCC, 1310.

26 See OC, 13.

27 See OC, 34.

28 See OC, 36.

Word at Mass on a weekday or a Sunday.[29] When Confirmation takes place at a Mass during certain solemnities or Sundays, the readings of that day take precedence. But this ceremony does not include Mass, so all the readings may be taken from the Lectionary's section for "Ritual Masses," no matter what day it is.

The conferral of Confirmation proceeds as it does at the celebration of Confirmation within Mass.[30] After the Universal Prayer, though, the liturgy goes immediately to the Lord's Prayer and concludes with the bishop's blessing.[31]

Even though the ceremony is shorter, it still brims with meaning. However, the relationship between Baptism, Confirmation, and Eucharist is harder to appreciate because the newly confirmed do not immediately receive Communion, and the fruits of the Spirit usher the candidates into the world without the fruits of the Eucharist.

2.   Who prepares the Confirmation liturgy?

Any number of individuals may prepare the Confirmation liturgy, but it would be best to learn from the bishop's office what he expects to take place. Often he has a master of ceremonies who will guide the preparation. Otherwise, the normal liturgy preparation team in the parish accepts the responsibility. This may include the pastor, the deacon, liturgist, musicians, sacristans, the youth minister, the catechists, and any others with a role to play. If the candidates are coming from several different parishes, representatives from each parish may wish to participate. Sometimes the people preparing for this occasion do not otherwise prepare events together. All need to be especially charitable, willing to listen to the ideas of others, and to offer suggestions that will advance the Gospel.

> If, however, the candidates for Confirmation are children who have not received the Most Holy Eucharist and are not being admitted to First Communion at this liturgical celebration or if other special circumstances so suggest, Confirmation should be conferred outside Mass.
>
> —*The Order of Confirmation*, 13

Communication is essential among these participants. The more everyone knows what others are doing the more smoothly the ceremony will go. The

---

29 See OC, 37.
30 See OC, 38–46.
31 See OC, 47–49.

arrival of the bishop usually inspires everyone to make a good impression—not just on him, but on all the visitors to the church.

3. If our candidates are multicultural, what language should we use for the liturgy?

Check out the USCCB's "Guidelines for a Multilingual Celebration of the Mass."[32] If the families and friends of the candidates speak languages other than English, it may be good to include those languages in the liturgy. In general, do not repeat sections of the Mass in multiple languages. Everything should be done once. The readings may each be proclaimed in a different language; if so, it would be courteous to provide a printed copy of the reading in the alternative language. The translation of the Scripture texts may be printed in the worship aid. That way all can participate better in the Liturgy of the Word.

The language of the homily will depend on the bishop's abilities and the presence of different groups throughout the congregation. Music from different ethnic traditions may be sung. A series of people may read the petitions of the Universal Prayer in their own tongues. If the petitions are read in multiple languages a translation should be included in the worship aid.

Whatever language was used for the catechesis of the candidates would logically be the language the bishop uses to confer

The language of the homily will depend on the bishop's abilities and the make-up of the congregation.

the sacrament. But as in all things, it is better to ask. Sensitivity to a multicultural presence will help make this a special celebration in which the manifold gifts of the Spirit, who speaks to the world in many tongues, will be evident in the gathering of the faithful.

---

32 This document can be found on the website of the United States Conference of Catholic Bishops: www.usccb.org/prayer-and-worship/the-mass/frequently-asked-questions/guidelines-for-a-multilingual-celebration-of-mass.cfm.

4.   How should the candidates dress?

The candidates should dress as they would for an important event. Some prefer formal wear, or at least business casual. However, some come from parishes where the economy is not strong, or the traditions of formality seem

Candidates may wear an alb.

relaxed by comparison with other locales. What candidates wear should indicate the seriousness with which they take the ceremony.

The Order of Confirmation makes no provision for ceremonial garments. Some parishes have provided alb and a red stole for candidates. Any baptized Christian could wear an alb, as servers do at Mass. But a stole is a garment reserved for deacons, priests, and bishops. It would be inappropriate for Confirmation candidates to vest in a stole, no matter what color.

5.   Does the liturgical year have an impact on the celebration?

Sometimes the liturgical year governs the choice of readings and prayers at a Confirmation Mass.[33] If the celebration takes place on any solemnity such as Sts. Peter and Paul on June 29, or on any Sunday of Advent, Lent, or Easter Time, the readings and prayers of that Mass take precedence. The same is true of the Octave of Easter—the first full week after Easter Sunday. If the Confirmation is taking place on the Wednesday after Easter, for example, the readings and prayers of that day take precedence of the Mass of Confirmation in the Missal and the Lectionary.

If the ceremony takes place during Lent, the church should be decorated in moderation. However, the Gloria should always be sung at a Confirmation Mass, even if it takes place during Advent or Lent. This differs from the Alleluia, which is always replaced with another Gospel Acclamation throughout every Mass of Lent.

The music for the celebration should also fit the liturgical year. If the celebration takes place during Easter Time, it would be appropriate to sing

---

33 See CB, Appendix III.

any Easter hymn, not just hymns for the Holy Spirit. The *Graduale Romanum* makes a few seasonal suggestions for the antiphons at Mass, as indicated in the appropriate places above, but these antiphons can always be replaced with other songs.

If the ceremony is taking place during Easter Time, the Paschal candle should be lighted as it is for every liturgy during the fifty days of Easter.

6. Should the Paschal candle be lighted whenever we celebrate Confirmation?

The Order of Confirmation makes no mention of the Paschal candle, but there are parishes where the candle has been lighted for Confirmation. The Paschal candle burns throughout the fifty days of Easter Time, and also for funerals and Baptisms. Because Confirmation is a sacrament of initiation like Baptism, some parishes light the Paschal candle to draw another connection between the two sacraments. But there is no mention of it in *The Order of Confirmation*.

7. What else should be kept in mind about the environment?

The church should look festive. This is one of the great sacraments of the church, one of the significant events in the parish's year of celebrations, and a turning point in the lives of the candidates and their families and sponsors.

Although the bishop is permitted to wear a white chasuble, he will probably wear red vesture, the same color the celebrant and deacon use for Pentecost and the occasional votive Mass of the Holy Spirit. On days of the calendar that outrank the Mass of Confirmation, such as a Sunday in Advent or Lent, he wears the color associated with that Mass. Many of those responsible for decorating the church choose red flowers and cloths that diffuse the liturgical color like so many tongues as of fire.

Otherwise, the usual basic rules apply. The Church prefers noble simplicity rather than ostentation, as well as authenticity and dignity.[34]

The vessel with chrism may be incorporated into the environment.

---

34 See the GIRM, 292.

Consequently the use of natural flowers and plants gathered from creation are always preferred to their artificial counterparts.

When working on the environment, decorators should keep in mind the actions of the liturgy. Before arranging the space, they should find out where the conferral of Confirmation will take place, and where the bishop, the candidates and the sponsors need to stand. In this way decorators can be sure to provide ample space for the movement of the participants.

8. Should we establish rules for photographers?

Probably. If you do not, photographers will boldly go where no one else has gone before. Seriously, how you set the rules for photographers is totally up to you. However, some parishes find it valuable to have a policy established for all such events—Baptisms, first Communions, *quinceañeras*, weddings, and Confirmations. Most photographers appreciate knowing the local rules, too.

For example, you may want to exclude a photographer's access to the sanctuary. You may prefer to have video cameras in place before the ceremony begins—and require that they remain stationary. You may restrict movement of photographers during the service so that they do not distract the liturgical action and the prayer of the people. Even though you set some rules, keep the tone positive. Most families will want a visual record of the ceremony, so the photographers are providing them a much-desired service.

Still, the liturgy is more important than the record of the liturgy. Welcome photographers. Invite them to participate in the celebration as believers. Encourage them to come back to your church sometime when they do not have to work, so that they can join the community in full, conscious, and active participation at the Mass.

9. What should we consider in regard to the music?

Promote congregational singing as much as possible. If you do not have much experience preparing music, be sure to consult with musicians in the parish and even in other parishes. Some choose songs that sound more youth-friendly on a recording than they do in the liturgy. Think about the music that people sing well, and be sure to include something of that repertoire. You will probably have a very unique assembly for this event—a lot of people who have never worshiped with one another before. Musicians should be prepared with music that fits the occasion but also invites the ready participation of those who have gathered for the event. A good songleader can make the community want to sing. Give them hymns and acclamations that will let them express their faith together in song.

Even if you do not regularly have a choir, you may find that assembling one for Confirmation is achievable. Many people who can sing do not wish to commit to regular responsibilities with a choir, but they will lend their voice to days such as Christmas, Easter, and the Confirmation liturgy. A good choir can sing a musical selection before the service

When selecting music for the Confirmation liturgy, consider music that not only fits the occasion but also invites assembly participation.

begins or at the Preparation of the Gifts or after Communion. They can inspire the entire assembly to sing congregational music by lending strong support.

You may consider rehearsing the congregation before the Mass begins. In this way the song leader can establish a rapport with the people and tell them how important their singing will be. By practicing some of the lesser-known musical pieces, you extend hospitality to the people who have gathered by helping them participate with heart and voice.

If multiple ethnicities are represented in the congregation, you may include a variety of music that will help each one feel at home at some point in the ceremony. You may need more than one choir in the church to make this work, but ethnic groups are often honored to be asked to sing. Many of them will bring to the celebration new measures of professionalism and diversity.

10. Who prepares the petitions for the Universal Prayer?

Suggested petitions are included in *The Order of Confirmation.*[35] These include a petition each for the newly confirmed, their parents and sponsors, the Church, and the world. However, you are not restricted to using them. They may inspire you to compose your own or give you a base from which you can add or replace petitions in that set.

---

35 See OC, 30.

If you have someone in the community with the gift of crafting prayers, this is a perfect opportunity for that person to create the petitions for the confirmation ceremony. Such petitions can be concrete, local, and inspiring.

As part of their catechetical preparation, candidates may contribute intentions that they wish to have included in the Confirmation Mass. It may be impossible to include all the petitions they would like to have, or to use precisely the wording that candidates submit. Nonetheless, seeing a list of concerns could inspire someone who can write petitions to author a set that takes into consideration the prayers of the candidates themselves.

The composition of the Universal Prayer enjoys great freedom, but there are a few guideposts to keep in mind. The prayers should include the needs of the Church, public authorities and the salvation of the whole world, those burdened by any kind of difficulty, and the local community.[36] Catechists could ask candidates during their preparation, what do they think the Church needs? What prayers should this community say for public authorities? What petitions, if granted, would advance the salvation of the whole world? Who is most burdened by difficulty? What does their local community need right now? What do they hope to accomplish with the gifts of the Spirit that they will receive in this sacrament? Making the petitions local and current will add life to them, and the candidates are well positioned to enhance the significance of these prayers.

Celebrating the Liturgy

1.   What is *The Roman Pontifical*?

The Roman Pontifical is a book that scripts the principal liturgical celebrations over which a bishop presides. It includes the Rite of the Dedication of a Church, the Rites of Ordination, and the Order of Confirmation. The Catholic Church has had a book like this for many centuries, but it has continually needed updating. For many years after the Second Vatican Council a complete Roman Pontifical did not exist as a single book in English. The ceremonies were published independently. In 2012, however, the orders of service that a bishop needs were gathered into a single book in time for the Chrism Mass with its new translation.

---

36 See GIRM, 70.

The newly retranslated *Order of Confirmation* in English is now published as a separate book in the United States together with the Spanish translation. This makes it convenient for a bishop to use in a country where many confirmations use both languages. The revised English translation makes the 2012 *Roman Pontifical* slightly out of date. Most parishes do not own a *Roman Pontifical*, but the bishop and pertinent diocesan offices will have one.

2. What makes the revised English translation of *The Order of Confirmation* different from the first one?

The new translation takes into account some of the revisions made to *The Roman Missal* in 2011. For example, the presidential prayers of the Confirmation Mass (the Collect, the Prayer over the Offerings, the Preface, the Prayer after Communion, the Solemn Blessing and the Prayer over the People) all received new English translations in 2011, so they needed to be copied into *The Order of Confirmation* itself.

Furthermore, one of the familiar responses the people make at Mass changed from "And also with you" to "And with your spirit." The Confirmation candidates now use the words from the revised response as the bishop anoints each of them with chrism.

The Code of Canon Law was revised after the first *Rite of Confirmation* was published, so a few adjustments had to be made to keep the books synchronized. For example, parents now may not replace sponsors and present their own children for Confirmation. *The Lectionary for Mass* also had a couple of very minor variations from the ritual book, such as the sequence of the fourth and fifth Gospel Acclamations. All these matters have been addressed to make the book more current.

In the end, people will not notice much of a difference. Perhaps the most striking difference is in the Confirmation prayer itself, which names the gifts of the Holy Spirit. These now use the same translation as the *Catechism of the Catholic Church*, which will unify catechesis with liturgical celebration.

The ceremony itself has not changed since the book was first published in Latin in 1971. The first version of the post–Vatican II Confirmation book has remained remarkably current for the needs of the Church today.

3. How should the candidates be involved in the liturgy?

The primary role of the candidates is to get confirmed. In some parishes the candidates take roles as liturgical ministers or singers. However, others can provide those ministries for this ceremony, and in a way they should. The entire community should be involved as much as possible.

If the candidates are very young, this may further limit what they are capable of doing. Nonetheless, *The Order of Confirmation* suggests that the newly confirmed may join in the procession of the gifts,[37] and they may do this regardless of their age.

4. How should we prepare persons with disabilities?

All baptized, unconfirmed Catholics who have the use of reason are candidates for Confirmation. Some persons with developmental or mental disabilities may never attain the use of reason, but the bishops of the United States of America urge that they receive Confirmation at the appropriate time.[38] They may make their preparation for this sacrament as they are able, in whatever manner the parish or diocese can help. The inclusion of persons with disabilities in the ceremony is another sign that the sacrament is less about the accomplishments of the candidates and more about the gifts of the Spirit.

5. How do we explain our Communion policy to guests who are not Catholic?

The United States Conference of Catholic Bishops issued guidelines for the reception of Communion in 1996. They can be accessed here: www.usccb .org/prayer-and-worship/the-mass/order-of-mass/liturgy-of-the-eucharist /guidelines-for-the-reception-of-communion.cfm.

This is the simplest way to handle the delicate matter of who receives Communion at a Catholic Mass. The norms explain how Catholics should prepare for Communion, clarify why other Christians do not participate in

---

37 See OC, 31.

38 See *Guidelines for the Celebration of the Sacraments with Persons with Disabilities*, 16.

Communion at a Catholic Mass, give advice for those not receiving Communion, and offer an extension of friendship to those who are not Christian.

If you are preparing a printed worship aid for the celebration, you may include the norms from the American bishops. If you keep a hymnal or worship aid in the pew of your church, the guidelines are probably printed there already.

If you think it better to make a verbal announcement, a deacon or catechist could take on the responsibility in the introductory remarks before the Mass begins. The wording would best imitate the style of the guidelines published by the American bishops. The welcome at the start of the ceremony should truly make people feel appreciated and at home. The prayers of all will be needed.

6.   Whatever happened to the Confirmation slap?

Durandus, a thirteenth-century French bishop of Mende, introduced a slap in the Confirmation ceremony. At the time, bishops also presided over the ceremony for making new knights, and the slap appeared in that ritual as well. The new recruit could thus demonstrate his willingness to endure all difficulties in defense of his country.

In his Confirmation ceremony, Durandus had the bishop strike the face of the newly confirmed. He thought that this would accomplish a number of things—it would help the person remember that he or she was confirmed, it would demonstrate the strengthening of one's faith, it would represent the imposition of hands, and it would frighten and drive out the evil spirit. Because the bishop delivered the slap while saying, "Peace be with you," it also expressed the kiss of peace.[39]

The slap was removed from the ceremony after the Second Vatican Council because the liturgical reformers thought no one understood the meaning of the rite.[40] Today after anointing the candidate while placing his hand on the candidate's head, the bishop says, "Peace be with you." This often becomes a sign of peace, a much more appropriate sign between a bishop and a member of his flock.

---

39 See the CD in *Ages of Initiation*, chapter 8, section 10.
40 See Consilium Study Group 26, Schemata 285, 4 April 1968.

7.   Where is the record of Confirmation kept?

The record of Confirmation is normally kept in the archives of the parish where the ceremony took place. Other options are possible, such as a diocesan archive.[41] In ceremonies where candidates from more than one parish were confirmed, records may be kept in multiple locations. When in doubt, record the Confirmation where it took place and also in any other place where people may go looking for it. It could be helpful many years later when a person needs to obtain proof of Confirmation in order to enter a religious community, be ordained, or serve as a godparent. A Catholic is to be confirmed before getting married if Confirmation can be administered without grave inconvenience.[42] Some dioceses require Confirmation before Marriage because they feel they can conveniently offer adults the opportunity they need.

The record should include the features one would expect: the names of the confirmed, the minister, the parents, the sponsors, and the place and date of the ceremony.[43]

The parish must send a record of Confirmation to the church of Baptism of each candidate.[44] This will be added to that person's baptismal record. When a Catholic wishes to be married, he or she will need to provide an updated baptismal certificate. The original certificate will tell where the baptism took place, but the person needs to contact that church for an updated record because it keeps the complete file of sacraments such as Baptism, Confirmation, and Marriage. Years after the ceremony, if a person who was confirmed has difficulty obtaining a copy of the Confirmation certificate or locating the parish where the ceremony took place, the church of Baptism should have the pertinent information.

8.   After the Confirmation Mass, what do we do?

Rejoice that the Holy Spirit has come into the hearts of the faithful. Celebrate with a reception. Visit with the bishop. Pose for photos. Thank God for the ministry that the newly confirmed will now be offering to the Church and the world.

---

41 See CCL, 895.
42 See CCL, 1065.
43 See OC, 14.
44 See OC, 15; see also CCL, 535 §2.

RESOURCES

Church Documents

- *Catechism of the Catholic Church.* 2nd ed. Washington, DC: United States Confirmation of Catholic Bishops, 1997. Summary of Catholic Church teaching, including a major section on the sacraments.
- *Ceremonial of Bishops.* Collegeville, Minnesota: The Liturgical Press, 1989. Rubrics and commentary that the bishop needs for ceremonies over which he presides.
- *The Order of Confirmation.* Washington, DC: United States Conference of Catholic Bishops, 2015. The official liturgical book for the Confirmation ceremony.
- *The Rite of Baptism for Children.* Washington, DC: United States Conference of Catholic Bishops, 1970. The official liturgical book for the Baptism of infants and young children.
- *Rite of Christian Initiation of Adults.* Chicago, Illinois: Liturgy Training Publications, 1988. The official liturgical book for the initiation of adults and children of catechetical age. Their initiation includes Confirmation.

Theological and Historical Resources

- Denysenko, Nicholas E. *Chrismation: A Primer for Catholics.* Collegeville, Minnesota: Liturgical Press, 2014. A clear explanation of the Eastern Orthodox practice of chrismation, written especially for Catholics who want a better understanding.
- Gabrielli, Timothy R. *Confirmation: How a Sacrament of God's Grace Became All about Us.* Collegeville, Minnesota: Liturgical Press, 2013. A careful and useful analysis of cultural influences on the theology of Confirmation in the twentieth century.

- *Receive the Gift: The Age of Confirmation; A Resource Guide for Bishops.* Washington, DC: United States Conference of Catholic Bishops, 2004. A discussion aid to help bishops establish the age of Confirmation in their diocese.

- Turner, Paul. *Ages of Initiation: The First Two Christian Millennia.* Collegeville, Minnesota: The Liturgical Press, 2000. The history of the age of the candidates for Confirmation and first Communion, as well as the history of the sequence of those two sacraments.

- _____. *Confirmation: The Baby in Solomon's Court.* Chicago, Illinois: Hillenbrand Books, 2006. An analysis of seven different models of Confirmation and the implications behind their multiplicity.

- _____. *The Hallelujah Highway: A History of the Catechumenate.* Chicago, Illinois: Liturgy Training Publications, 2000. Easy-to-read overview of the development of the catechumenate from its apostolic beginnings to its post–Vatican II restoration.

Pastoral Resources

- *Come, Holy Spirit.* Chicago, Illinois: Liturgy Training Publications, 2001. A prayer book for those preparing to be confirmed.

- Fitzgerald, Timothy. *Confirmation: A Parish Celebration*, revised. Chicago, Illinois: Liturgy Training Publications, 1990. A practical guide to celebrating the sacrament in your parish.

- Gallagher, Patrick. *Being a Sponsor: Sharing the Gift of Confirmation.* Chicago, Illinois: Liturgy Training Publications. A helpful guide for Confirmation sponsors.

- Mick, Lawrence E. *Forming the Assembly to Celebrate Sacraments.* Chicago, Illinois: Liturgy Training Publications, 2007. Tips for bringing the liturgical assembly's prayer alive.

- Nash, Dora. *Confirmed in the Faith: A Catholic Confirmation Course.* England: Gracewing, 2001. A Christocentric preparation for Confirmation. This book is distributed in the United States through Liturgy Training Publications.

- Turner, Paul. *Celebrating Initiation: A Guide for Priests*. Franklin Park, Illinois: World Library Publications, 2007. Suggestions for priests who preside over any of the initiation rites, including the circumstances when they confirm.

- _____. *A Simple Guide to Confirmation*. Washington, DC: Federation of Diocesan Liturgical Commissions, 2007. A very brief overview of the sacrament.

GLOSSARY

Apostolic See: The Church of Rome whose origins are traced to the Apostles. Also called the Holy See.

Baptismal Promises: The promises are vows made by the person being baptized or by the parents and godparents on behalf of the child. We renew our baptismal promises whenever we sign ourselves with holy water, on Easter Sunday, whenever the Sprinkling Rite takes place at Mass, and during the Confirmation liturgy.

Apostles' Creed: The ancient baptismal statement of the Church's faith. The questions used in the celebration of Baptism correspond to the statements of the Apostles' Creed. It may be used as the Profession of Faith at Mass, and is particularly appropriate during Lent and Easter Time.

Catechumen: An unbaptized person who has declared their intention to prepare for the sacraments of initiation and has been accepted into the order of catechumens. Catechumens, though not yet fully initiated, are joined to the Church and are considered part of the household of Christ. The names of those accepted as catechumens are to be written in the register of catechumens kept by the parish.

Catechetical Age: Usually considered to be seven years of age; also called the age of reason or the age of discretion. For the purpose of Christian initiation, a person who has reached catechetical age is considered an adult and is to be initiated into the Church according to the *Rite of Christian Initiation of Adults* and catechized according to his or her needs. A person baptized after having reached the age of reason is to receive all three sacraments of initiation. Before this age, the person is considered an infant and is baptized using the *Rite of Baptism for Children*.

Character: The indelible sign of the Holy Spirit received at Confirmation in order to publicly give witness to the Good News of Jesus Christ.

Chrism: One of the three Holy Oils. It is consecrated by the bishop at the Chrism Mass and used at the Baptism of infants, at Confirmation, at the ordination of priests and bishops, and at the dedication of churches and altars. Chrism is scented, usually with balsam, which creates a distinctive and pleasing aroma; it is the only one of the three sacramental oils that is scented. Chrism is stored in the ambry and in oil stocks that are often labeled SC, for "Sacred Chrism."

Evangelization: To bring "the Good News of Jesus into every human situation and seeking to convert individuals and society by the divine power of the Gospel itself."[1] Refer also to "New Evangelization" below.

Hand Laying (Imposition of Hands): A gesture of blessing or invocation mentioned in the New Testament in conjunction with prayer (for example, Acts 13:3; 2 Timothy 1:6). The gesture is performed by extending both hands forward with the palms turned downward. Depending on the circumstances, the hands may be placed on the person's head or stretched out over a group of people or over an object. The gesture is used in many of the sacraments to indicate the conferral of special grace or the invocation of the Holy Spirit, as at Ordination and Confirmation, during absolution in the Sacrament of Penance, at the invocation of the Spirit during a Eucharistic Prayer. The same gesture is also used during a Solemn Blessing or Prayer over the People at the conclusion of Mass.

Gradual: A name used at times to refer to the psalm sung or proclaimed after the First Reading at Mass.

Graduale Romanum (The Roman Gradual): The liturgical book that contains the chants of the Mass, along with their musical notation. Both the Ordinary and the Proper of the Mass are contained in this book.

Graduale Simplex (The Simple Gradual): The a liturgical book that contains simpler chants to be sung in place of the more complex melodies found in the Graduale Romanum.

New Evangelization: "The New Evangelization focuses specifically on those communities that have Catholic roots but have 'lost a living sense of faith, or even no longer consider themselves members of the Church.'"[2]

---

1 *Go and Make Disciples,* 10.

2 *Disicples Called to Witness,* p. 1; quoting *Redemptoris missio,* 33.